THE POWER OF BROKENNESS
...the language of healing

Making Healthy Choices That Change Our Lives, Hearts, And Families

Based on Biblical Principles

Glen Kerby and Jim McCraigh

Seventh Edition - Copyright © 2014-2024 by Glen Kerby and Jim McCraigh

All rights reserved. Except for limited quotation for the purposes of review, no part of this book may be reproduced or transmitted in any form or by any means, electronic or mechanical, including photocopying, recording, printing, digitization, or storage in any on-line database or retrieval system of any kind without the express written consent of the publisher at jmccraigh@gmail.com

This book should not be considered as the ultimate source of Biblical interpretation regarding the verses contained herein.

ISBN 13: 9781468123982

Printed in the United States of America

Note: The name of satan is not capitalized in this book. I have chosen not to acknowledge him in any way, even though it violates rules of grammar.

Rev 6.13.24247

This book is dedicated to the Spirit of God, my wife, the problems we have faced in our lives and our friendship for one another. Without God's inspiration, the pain of the past, the contribution and encouragement of my church family, friends, and the gifts of those who have come to support the effort of this ministry, there would be nothing to dedicate. May it be a blessing to you!

SUBSCRIBE TO JIM'S BLOG (FREE):
https://theamericanfaithandfreedomblog.substack.com/
Or scan this QR code…

For a leader's guide about conducting a Power of Brokenness Group Study, see the end of this book.

For Discounted Bulk Orders go to or scan:
https://theamericanfaithandfreedomblog.substack.com/p/jims-books

Table of Contents

1 Life 5

2 Seek 16

3 Trust 26

4 Fearless 36

5 Forgiven 44

6 Transform 58

7 Miracle 68

8 Relationship 74

9 Community 82

10 Vigilance 92

11 Power 98

12 Share 104

Final Thoughts. 112

Serenity Prayer 113

Leader's Guide. 114

Introduction

As we struggle to find answers in difficult times, certain words can take on entirely new meanings for us. In this study, we will explore twelve such words that people of faith use every day. We will see how they relate to the process of growing closer to God through the power of Jesus Christ. These words of healing are for all of us who are sick and tired of anything that may be destroying our lives. They are for all of us who want to stop living in fear, anxiety, emotional pain, shame, or guilt. They are for all of us who want to separate ourselves from the issues of the past. These words are for all of us who want to start over again with the help of a loving God who will forgive us.

At the same time, words can also be easily misunderstood. Confusing the meaning of these words can separate us from understanding truth and our fellow believers. This can cause us to have difficulty with communicating our faith and struggles with one another. It is our hope that this study will help you find the right words to share your experience, strength, and hope with others or that you will better understand others as they share theirs with you!

Since the beginning, language has been one of God's most powerful ways of communicating with us. Expressions like, "God's Word" or Christ is "the Word having become flesh" are vital to our understanding of God and seeking His truth. *There is nothing more powerful than God's living word and Holy Spirit when we seek answers to life's problems.*

Our hope is that this study will help you to strengthen your faith and grow closer to Him. The process of healing and recovery is the process of restoration through Jesus Christ. No matter where we are in our own journey, one day or 25 years, these are the words that will help strengthen our Christian faith and point us towards the victorious life that God intends for each of us.

Glen Kerby and Jim McCraigh

Other Books by Jim McCraigh…

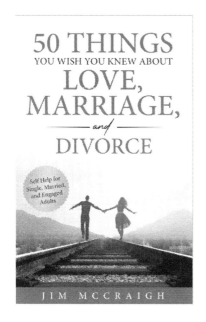

https://amzn.to/4aWQJAe

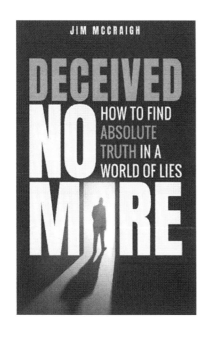

https://amzn.to/4bLQARj

*^{22}But when the Holy Spirit controls our lives, he will produce this kind of
fruit in us: love, joy, peace, patience, kindness, goodness, faithfulness,
^{23}gentleness, and self-control. Here there is no conflict with the law. ^{24}Those
who belong to Christ Jesus have nailed the passions and desires of their sinful nature
to his cross and crucified them there. ^{25}If we are living now by the Holy Spirit, let us
follow the Holy Spirit's leading in every part of our lives. ^{26}Let us
not become conceited, or irritate one another, or be jealous of one another.
(Galatians 5:22-2)*

Please Leave an Amazon Review if You Liked this Book!

If you enjoyed this book, it would be greatly appreciated if you left a review on Amazon so that others can receive the same benefits as you have. Your review will help me see what is working and what is not so I can better serve you and others... Simply go to:

https://amzn.to/3RcCtME
Or scan this QR Code:

Brokenness is the acknowledgment of grace where self-will is superseded by God's will. While righteousness demands payment for evil done, brokenness recognizes that payment cannot be made regardless of our human effort and rejoices in the forgiveness of sin...

life

we admit that apart from God, we were personally powerless over our behaviors and thoughts and that our lives had become unmanageable...

Read: John 10:10 (That you may have life)

life: noun (Dictionary): the present state of existence; the time from birth to death
(Faith): that which breathes, the breathing substance or being; the giving of a soul by the creator; the inner being of a person; the raising of something from death

"recovery"
The formal process of dealing with the issues in our lives that create the symptoms that cause us to live lives that are less than what God has intended for us.

A fuel truck driver was on a delivery run during a raging blizzard in the days before CB radios and cell phones. While traveling along a dark, deserted stretch between two isolated towns, the truck skidded off the road and wound up hopelessly stuck. As the storm passed and sunrise came, the temperature dropped to nearly 40° below zero. The driver stayed with the truck in the hope that someone would pass by and rescue him. After several hours of waiting, he ran out of diesel fuel. Without the engine running, the truck's heater was useless. When police found him later the next day, he had frozen to death.

This kind of tale is not uncommon in the northern parts of Canada. It seems that hardly a winter goes by that someone isn't lost. The thing that makes this story so remarkable is that the driver had nearly 10,000 gallons of diesel fuel in the tanker he was hauling. At first glance it would seem there was no way to move it from the tanker into the truck in order to keep it running. But when we heard this story, I immediately thought that there must have been some way to do that. The driver could have saved his life if he would have just tried something... anything! If he would have just focused his energy on using the resources that he had in the situation in which he found himself, he would have survived.

Many of us find ourselves in the same type of place. Something (our behavior, our actions, our spirit, or a relationship) is killing us and forcing us into a decision between life and death. There is an answer close at hand, but it seems impossible for us to reach. We try to gain some comfort in the cab of our truck, even though our heart tells us that it is a place of death. We have hopes that someone will come and rescue us, or that our situation will somehow change by itself. For many of us, the fear of what we will find if we do choose the things life is greater than the pain of the issues we struggle with now. Meanwhile, things of death multiply and choke us while we wonder if the things of life are beyond our grasp.

Denial is a self-protecting behavior that kills us spiritually. To begin to heal, we must admit the problems we face for what they are. We need to see that the emotional pain we are in right now can become one of the most valuable assets we'll ever have.

Working to overcome our struggles will help us establish a closer relationship with the God who loves us. It will also help us meet our own needs and those of our family and others around us in a healthier way. When we begin to realize that we have no one else to call upon except the Power who created us, our life will begin to change. When we make the choice between life and death by genuinely crying out to God for help, we will come to know that we can have hope. Jeremiah, the author of the book of Lamentations, also saw a time of incredible personal struggle. It was in the midst of all his pain that God spoke to him about what was to come:

> *[19] The thought of my suffering and homelessness is bitter beyond words. [20] I will never forget this awful time, as I grieve over my loss. [21] Yet I still dare to hope when I remember this: [22] The unfailing love of the LORD never ends! By his mercies we have been kept from complete destruction. [23] Great is his faithfulness; his mercies begin afresh each day. [24] I say to myself, "The LORD is my inheritance; therefore, I will hope in him!" [25] The LORD is wonderfully good to those who wait for him and seek him. (Lamentations 3:19-25)*

True and lasting healing begins only when we cry out to God for help. When we do so, God will find us, direct us, deliver us, and walk with us into a new life that is so full of promise that we may even doubt at times whether we are worthy of it! Be assured that *you are* worthy of a life that is filled with love, joy, and peace. These are promises given to us by the greatest authority in all the universe, and they cannot be taken away from us as people of faith. (See John 10.) When we call out to God for help, we have already begun to spiritually overcome the denial that has kept us from being truly His.

Some of us may have thought that we had already made this choice to trust in the promise of God. But somehow, the things of the world, the ideas of religion, the pain of life, the injury, the fear, the guilt, or the shame have all worked together to try to steal that promise away from us. For others, we have gone through life taking what we needed and living by whatever rules we invented to survive. But, when we finally do admit that our choices are not working, we can begin to see that there *is* hope in Christ. Then, we'll begin to see how we can trust in the real promise of God in a way that we never before thought possible!

No matter how large or small our issues seem today... the depression, fear, anxiety, anger, pornography, gambling, relational failure, or the pain of grief, shame, guilt, food, work, isolation, or codependency... such things can only lead us into deeper pain tomorrow. Out of control pain leads to the breakdown of trust and relationships with family and friends. Unfettered gossip, complaining and grumbling serves only to injure others. The anguish of divorce or grief doesn't get any better without admitting our pain, dealing with it and then finding help to fight off future bitterness and resentment. Unbridled religious foolishness will only lead to increased pain in our own lives and in those around us. Using the Bible to beat up others so that we don't have to deal with our own issues only brings greater personal destruction in the end.

Denial in admitting our own problems and issues stalls our healing and hampers our spiritual growth. With denial comes the ever-present temptation to disregard the root cause of our symptoms and leads only to more failed attempts at superficial change. When in denial, our hope is based on the false notion that things will change for the better only if we take control of things ourselves. It is the choice for the things of death.

Denial is universal in the human experience. Very few of us have not struggled to admit the truth about our lives. For a person trying to overcome their denial, it can feel like one of the most difficult things they have ever had to do, despite the overwhelming evidence that surrendering the garbage of our past lives is a good thing. Being open to God's voice is the first step down a life changing path. But how do we get there?

> *¹My child, listen to me and treasure my instructions. ²Tune your ears to wisdom and concentrate on understanding. ³Cry out for insight and understanding. ⁴Search for them as you would for lost money or hidden treasure. ⁵Then you will understand what it means to fear the LORD, and you will gain knowledge of God. ⁶For the LORD grants wisdom! From his mouth come knowledge and understanding. ⁷He grants a treasure of good sense to the godly. He is their shield, protecting those who walk with integrity. ⁸He guards the paths of justice and protects those who are faithful to him. ⁹Then you will understand what is right, just, and fair, and you will know how to find the right course of action every time.*
> *(Proverbs 2:1-9)*

"denial"
self-protecting behavior that keeps us from honestly facing the truth about ourselves with God and others

We always have the opportunity to hold up a white flag and call off the whole war. But it isn't the waving of the white flag that is painful, it is everything that leads up to the decision to surrender that is difficult. Overcoming denial is often the greatest decision point in the life of anyone who has faced it. It is important to separate the pain of coming to the place of admitting our shortcomings from actually making our choice between life and death. Pretending it's OK for us to not make this choice leads only to us choosing death.

We can stop the behaviors and still be hopelessly lost. We can stop acting out with in our anger, pornography, food, drugs, alcohol, or codependency and falsely believe that we are in control of our situation. We can be a person who has given up on guilt, fixing others, perfectionism, or gambling, but still spend time gossiping or complaining about the awful condition of our lives, family, or church. If we simply stop the behaviors, we'll likely remain just as lost as we have ever been. This is because the ways in which we choose to act out are simply symptoms of much bigger problems. This is exactly why we need to admit our powerlessness over these things of death and instead choose the things of life.

The decision to overcome denial is a decision to seek healing. If we want to get better, we can. If we want to remain in the place of pain where we are now, we can do that too. The decision is ours. God wants a relationship with us. He will stand at our door and knock until our last breath on this planet.

> [20] *Here I am! I stand at the door and knock. If anyone hears my voice and opens the door, I will come in and eat with him, and he with me. (Revelation 3:20)*

The stark contrast between this way of thinking and how the world likes to handle problems is why the authors of this book believe this verse was divinely inspired. The world says… build up the individual, the answer is already within you and that self-help solutions work. God's way is to create strength through admission of weakness; power through confessing brokenness and victory through surrender to Him. These are not human ideas!

Recognizing and overcoming denial

How do you know if you are in denial? Ask yourself these questions and write your answers below:

1. Has your relationship with God been damaged by things that you have been doing?

_____

_____

_____

_____

2. Has your ability to serve others in need been compromised by what you are doing, (or been done to you)?

_____

_____

_____

_____

3. Do you believe that what you are struggling with has made you angry or come between you and God?

_____

_____

_____

_____

_____

4. Has what you are struggling with come between you and your family?

_____

_____

_____

_____

_____

"shame"

self-condemning thoughts that create a desire for us to avoid any subject, group, counseling, or assistance that will force us to admit our own failures

5. Have your struggles caused you to neglect responsibilities at home or at work?

_____

_____

_____

_____

_____

If you can say yes to any of the questions on the last page, you have a clear life or death choice to make. If you're not doing anything about the problem, you are in denial. Denial is a self-imposed prison. But if you face the truth, you can escape!

When we know better and continue acting out (engage in destructive behaviors), we are truly in denial and rebelling against God. Living in anger, bitterness, loneliness, and pain never leads to peace or freedom. When in denial, we often face feelings of being out of control, failure, loneliness, and inability to relate to others. This leaves us fighting a spiritual battle in our own strength.

The desire to look outside of ourselves for comfort comes from who God created us to be. We are hard-wired find our worth, not in ourselves alone, but as a child of God! But, more times than not, we get stuck somewhere between God and ourselves. Rather than pursuing a relationship with Him, we start substituting other things that we can control. These include people, places, and things; hanging on to past behaviors; hoping things will get better on their own or simply blaming others. Such things are steppingstones to spiritual death.

People, places, and things

A former participant in one of our small groups relates the following about the two years before he entered recovery:

> "I managed to move five times within four different cities. I was constantly looking for a better stereo system, a better car, a better girlfriend, a better city, or a new career. I wanted to find anything that would help me make more money, go to more parties, or meet more friends… anything that could help to distract me from the real problem. I was living a lie that had no end. Every day I was looking to fill myself up by acting out in my narcotics addiction. I suffered endless shame and guilt; endured constant turmoil and felt ongoing physical, emotional, and spiritual pain… But I still remained in denial that I had a problem, and the things of death had a hold on my life."

You don't have to be addicted to alcohol or narcotics for your spirit to be slowly and painfully dying. It can be a failure to admit problems with things like loneliness, isolation, depression, fear, codependency, rage, compulsive spending, overeating, religion or lust. Such dependence on people, places and things usually comes from a desire to minimize our problems or to blame others for our own shortcomings…

- It's only a problem when "they" are around
- He drinks way more than I do and nobody bothers him
- I only bet on weekends
- Lots of people have affairs
- I can't get away from the people that I act out with
- This city depresses me, no wonder I have this problem
- If only he would stop treating me that way
- I am the only person in this church who really understands God
- I hate (fill in the blank) because of what they have done to me.

Hanging on to the things of death

Have you ever watched a friend or relative suffering in a relationship that you knew was bad for them, but they couldn't seem to break free from it? You saw them suffer through all the arguments, the chaos, and the pain, but wondered why they chose not to escape from it? The answer is that the relationship was satisfying something so deep inside of them, that no matter how crazy that may seem, they were then more comfortable with the things of death than with the things of life.

We stay in denial in much the same way. We drink dirty water to quench a never-ending thirst that we have, as polluted as that water may be. But we are thirsty and that is the only kind of water that we can conceive of. We don't hope for something better because we don't really believe that there is such a thing. We think… "People don't really live that way. They are all as screwed up as I am... but they just have the ability or resources to pretend better than I can." We will stay stuck in that muddy, stagnant water until we understand that there is a different place to drink from that is clear, cold, fresh, and alive. But even the offer of such fresh water brings with it a struggle.

> *³⁷On the last day, the climax of the festival, Jesus stood and shouted to the crowds, "If you are thirsty, come to me! ³⁸If you believe in me, come and drink! For the Scriptures declare that rivers of living water will flow out from within." ³⁹(When he said, "living water," he was speaking of the Spirit, who would be given to everyone believing in him. But the Spirit had not yet been given, because Jesus had not yet entered into his glory.) ⁴⁰When the crowds heard him say this, some of them declared, "This man surely is the Prophet." ⁴¹Others said, "He is the Messiah." Still others said, "But he can't be! Will the Messiah come from Galilee? ⁴²For the Scriptures clearly state that the Messiah will be born of the royal line of David, in Bethlehem, the village where King David was born." ⁴³So the crowd was divided in their opinion about him. ⁴⁴And some wanted him arrested, but no one touched him. (John 7:37-44)*

"codependent"
Seeking, to be fulfilled, personal identity or approval from others at the expense of our personal well-being or our relationship with God.

God often uses water as an illustration in both the Old and New Testament. In this case, He asks us to reject the past and the places we've gone before to quench our thirst. *He wants us to come to Him instead.* God has something great in store for us. He invites us to reject the polluted waters of our past lives, and all of the foolishness that filthy water brings, and accept His offer instead.

"Everything will be better tomorrow"

In the midst of our pain, it's easy to buy into the lie that today's mistakes will be repaired by tomorrow's actions. People in recovery learn the expression "one day at a time" early in their experience. This comes straight from the advice of Christ.

> *"So don't worry about tomorrow, for tomorrow will bring its own worries. Today's trouble is enough for today. That "one day" is not tomorrow… and it is not yesterday… it is TODAY! (Matthew 6:34)*

satan* wants to defeat us in overcoming our denial by choosing the battle ground on which we wage war with him. If he can fight with us in the past or in the future, then we lose the battle to be liberated from things of death. If he can convince us to put off decisions that we need to make today in the hope that things will be better tomorrow, we will fail. If we accept a lifestyle where we endure the pain of today in the false hope that we will somehow do it differently tomorrow, we will never achieve the freedom that we desire.

To live lives of true peace, our only option is to make the decision to make today count. God wants us to make this the moment that we admit our brokenness and step out of our denial. This is the only moment in which He can minister to us… not yesterday or next week. He can forgive us for the past if we accept His Son and ask for His forgiveness. God promises to provide for us in the future if we seek to live within His will in the present.

> ***And don't worry about food – what to eat and drink. Don't worry whether God will provide it for you. (Luke 12:29)***

God wants us to live in the moment, where we can be empowered by Him to let go of the damage of the past and to give up worry about tomorrow. All we have to do is be willing to come to Him without denial and admit our powerlessness and let Him begin the new life that He has waiting for us.

Barriers to choosing

Being faced with this choice often leads to feelings of resentment and anger. Given enough time, this anger will turn itself against the very person who harbors it. The eventual result of this is often depression and feelings of worthlessness. In its worst form, it can lead to physical illness or even thoughts of suicide in some individuals.

Often, in the midst of anger, we often begin to look for a scapegoat. Who can we blame for our issues? We can direct our hate at those who have attacked or injured us... parents, spouses, relatives, employers, brothers, sisters, teachers or even strangers. We can also blame the church, religion, pastors, priests, or anyone else who we believe should have met our needs but didn't. In the midst of our angry denial, we can eventually come to blame God. We begin to envision Him as a cosmic killjoy who is forever torturing us. We can come to see Him as some sort of uncooperative genie in a bottle who did not come out to give us our three wishes and make things better. We often can make Him the target of our anger so we can rationalize the consequences of our own decisions by blaming Him for His lack of care and compassion. When we are willing to come out of our denial by admitting that we have a part in all of this, then we begin to heal.

Our response in spiritual death

Here, we often invent a god that we can blame for how messed up we are (religion); or we create a new god for ourselves a god of our own understanding… a composite of many man-made belief systems (such as New Age); or we simply deny the relevance or

---

* The name of satan is purposely not capitalized throughout this book.

existence of God (atheism). In each case, there is one common denominator... our will or logic becomes used to supersede the will of a loving and caring God in our life. We either put Him in a religious box, adding or subtracting attributes based on how we feel... or just ignore Him completely. No matter how you look at it, we are then manipulating God in an effort to stay in our denial and maintain control of our lives, other people, and circumstances.

Our response in eternal life

When we choose life, we clearly recognize the face of the things of death and reject them. We get out of the driver's seat and let Jesus take the wheel. When we stand aside from the pain of our lives controlled by fear, anger, and self-centeredness, we can come to recognize the spirit that is moving within us. Then, in that new life we can take what might be our first *real* look at who God is and what He wants for us. Paul wrote:

> *¹⁸I know that nothing good lives in me, that is, in my sinful nature. For I have the desire to do what is good, but I cannot carry it out. (Romans 7:18)*

This verse gives us a clear view of what is at stake in the decision to take the first step towards life. If we try to manage our own lives apart from God, we will be guided by the same nature that put us in the very mess that we are trying to get out of. Paul admits in this passage that he has the desire to do good, but that his weakness prevents even him from accomplishing it on his own.

This is not a "be good and God will love you" message. This is a "God loves you where you are right now" message. You belong to Him and He loves you and wants to walk with you, no matter what you have done, where you have been, what you have said or what you have thought. This is the good news... you are forgiven and God loves you through Christ. This is a message that needs to be taken to the end of the earth, and more than ever, needs to be clearly communicated in all Christian churches and fellowships. It doesn't matter what you have done or what has been done to you, all that matters is that you desire to have a relationship with Him. Christ came to tell us that God understands who we are, that He understands our nature and wants us to trust Him. He wants us to be forgiven and to give up the death of not being able to forgive others.

He wants to help us where we are today. He is not waiting for you to be perfect; he's not waiting for you to remove your tattoo, get a haircut, put on a suit, get a tie, or clean up your act. He is waiting for you to decide to walk away from the things of death so that He can take you to a new life. (Col 3:11) He can help us if we simply admit that we need help. He can give us answers if we admit that we don't have them ourselves. (Luke 11:9) He can carry the weight of it all if we tell Him it is too heavy. (Matthew 11:28) He can forgive our sins if we confess that we have them. (1 John 1:9)

In Romans Chapter 5, before Paul's revelation about his struggle to do good, he tells us the good news about overcoming his own bondage of denial to begin a lifetime of healing.

"guilt"
self-condemning thoughts that result from the realization that damage has been done to others or ourselves as a direct result of our personal actions

Take a look at the following verse:

> ⁶*While we were yet helpless, at the right time Christ died for the ungodly. Why, one will hardly die for a righteous man though perhaps for a good man one will dare even to die. But God shows His love for us in that while we were yet sinners Christ died for us. (Romans 5:6)*

In our journey of healing, as in our relationship with Christ, we don't need to start off perfect, we just need to be willing to choose the things life instead those of death!

More questions for reflection

6. In what areas of your life have you admitted your powerlessness? What scares you about giving up control?

_____
_____
_____
_____
_____

7. Could you now be in denial about any area(s) of your life?

_____
_____
_____
_____
_____

8. Have you seen the results of these self-defeating behaviors in your life?

9. Do you have a secret that you cannot share?

Devotional Verses

¹When the Lord brought back his exiles to Jerusalem;
it was like a dream!

²We were filled with laughter,
and we sang for joy.
And the other nations said,
"What amazing things the Lord has done for them."

³Yes, the Lord has done amazing things for us!
What joy!

⁴Restore our fortunes, Lord,
as streams renew the desert.

⁵Those who plant in tears
will harvest with shouts of joy.

⁶They weep as they go to plant their seed,
but they sing as they return with the harvest.

(Psalm 126)

seek

we came to believe that a power greater than ourselves could restore us to sanity...

Read: John 15:16 (You did not choose me, but I chose you)

seek: verb
(Dictionary): to make a search or inquiry
(Faith): to look for answers by moving our heart closer to God and taking a clear look at who He is

True seekers looking for answers come from a variety of backgrounds. Some don't know God and are looking for answers to the problems they face in everyday life. Others come from religious backgrounds but are still looking for answers for the pain of their lives. Finally, there are those who have been healing for some time and want to increase their understanding of who Christ is.

Each group brings unique perspectives to the table. One of the greatest things about this approach to seeking God is that we all start this relationship with Him in the same place. Nobody comes to the table with more than we do. God made everything, owns everything and has gifted each of us with the tools that we bring. Nobody can stand before God in an elevated or diminished position in comparison to any other individual. God does not care if you have been homeless and broken for 10 years or have and advanced degree in theology from Oxford. This reality allows us to consider our relationship with Jesus Christ from a position of brokenness. We need, (as we did in chapter one), to admit our powerlessness. We need to overcome the denial of the things that are destroying our lives, our peace, and our relationship with God. Without this honesty and brokenness, our knowledge means absolutely nothing.

In our walk of faith, our background is not what will help us to heal. True and complete healing comes from Christ. In many ways, those that come with what they believe to be superior knowledge and experience are more likely to struggle than those who can come to Christ in total brokenness. There are people with thirty years in church or thirty years in recovery who have never sought the truth needed to change their lives. Having knowledge and understanding truth are two completely different things.

> [7] ***The fear of the LORD is the beginning of knowledge, but fools despise wisdom and discipline. (Proverbs 1:7)***

We can't get to where we need to go if we can't move what we know from our heads to our hearts so that we can truly see who God is. This is because we need His power and strength to transform our lives.

"chips"

Coin-sized mementos given out at group meetings in celebration of milestones in one's recovery; (i.e.) 30 days of sobriety.

1. Are you truly open to seeking a truly intimate relationship with God? What, if anything is interfering with that?

_____

_____

_____

_____

_____

Seeking truth

An open and transparent search for answers requires willingness to look at two things:

Willingness to Believe in Something Bigger than Ourselves
For most of us, it is not difficult to believe that there is something larger than ourselves. We live in a universe that is infinitely large. The wonder of our own construction and the diversity of the living systems around us cannot simply be explained away as something accidental. Even the most hard-boiled, but intellectually honest scientist must concede that we are complex and intelligently designed beings.

In recovery, we seek truth in order to tear down the intellectual and spiritual roadblocks that keep us from understanding who God really is. The concept does not say we believe in a God who can restore us to sanity. *It says we came to believe.* Coming to believe requires intellectual honesty. It means that we must have a desire to seek the truth so we can fully believe in God.

Those who attempt to discount the existence of God often do so by trying to explain the origins of life as a mistake or accident. The probability of the complex life we see around us being an accident is about the same as the odds of a tornado going through a junk yard and creating an operational 747 aircraft from windswept rubbish.

No accident can make multiple working parts into a complex organism. The odds that even the most simple of elements could align themselves to produce the basic building blocks of life are one in 10 with 81 zeros after it! This represents a number so small that some say that it is smaller than zero. Even Darwin himself argued that if a system was made up of parts that could not function separated from one another, then his own theory of evolution would be disproved. The argument for the requirement of a creator is so compelling that it must remove any roadblock we might have in coming to believe in God.

One problem with science's ability to explain the origins of the universe (apart from God) revolve around our human inability to quantify something infinite. The vast majority of people worldwide believe that there is a God, but do not believe in absolute truth. How can you have an infinite God but not absolute truth? If you struggle with your belief in God, but still have a desire to understand the truth you are on the right track.

The important thing here is that we *came to believe*, not that we stumbled around in perpetual disbelief. If we want to believe in ourselves and return to our old way of life we can do that at any time. We have all seen the result of that belief system in our lives. What we need to ask ourselves is this... What do we want to be the driving force in our life, the power that created the universe and everything in it, or ourselves alone?

Willingness to Admit that How We Lived in the Past Was Insane
Admitting this takes us another step past overcoming denial. The very idea that self-help, self-direction, or self-centeredness can conquer the things that seek to control our lives is insanity. (The definition of insanity from a clinical standpoint is repetition of any action with a proven outcome with an expectation of different results.) This is where we prayerfully consider the things in our life that have led us to seek out help. If we are honest, we will see a clear pattern of undesirable actions and consequences.

If a husband tells his wife over and over again about what she needs to change in order for him to be "happy" and every time it turns into an argument that further destroys trust in the marriage, that is insanity.

If we are suffering with grief and find ourselves struggling with feelings of loneliness and depression, but deal with the symptoms by repeatedly isolating ourselves, by not answering the telephone, not leaving the house, or not reaching out to the people who want to help us and therefore slip into even greater pain, that is insanity.

If we enable someone else's bad behavior (acting in a codependent manner) and it is hurting both of us, but still we continue, that is insanity.

If we deal with pressure and guilt by drinking, overworking, isolating, overeating, substance abuse or using pornography and creating even greater guilt and pressure because if it, that is insanity.

If we live with guilt and shame brought about through self-condemnation and feel even more guilt because of it, that is insanity.

"brokenness"

living in the open admission that we are not God, but sinners who need the forgiveness of God through our savior Jesus Christ

2. Is there anything in your past or present that you would now classify as insane behavior?

_____

_____

_____

_____

How do we fix it? By seeking the God who created everything, who values us, who loves us and who has a plan for our lives. We fix it by seeking the Lord God who will forgive us for everything that we have ever done or ever will do. We fix it by placing our will and our lives in the hands of His only Son, Jesus Christ. We fix it by coming to Him with all that we have and seek to understand who He is. We begin fixing it when we can trust Him for the solutions to our problems. Only then can we stop living our lives in cycles of insanity.

Biblical reference

Matthew writes:

> *⁸For everyone who asks receives; he who seeks finds; and to him who knocks, the door will be opened. (Matthew 7:8)*

What is he telling us in this passage?
1.) It's all about seeking God
2.) If you seek Him, you will find Him
3.) When you find Him, He will respond
4.) He will give you the answers that you search for in life

In Chapter 2 of Philippians, the apostle Paul writes this:

> *¹²Therefore, my dear friends, as you have always obeyed—not only in my presence, but now much more in my absence—continue to work out your salvation with fear and trembling. (Philippians 2:12)*

Here Paul is asking the church to do something specific in his absence. He is saying I have been with you but I cannot be with you always and your salvation needs to be understood or worked out in your own mind with the utmost urgency, priority, and respect.

This is not about snappy sermons, self-help books or how many hours you spend memorizing Bible verses. It has to do with an honest understanding of who God is. It has to do with knowing that His Son was willing to die for us to remove our sin so that we could have an immediate and eternal relationship with Him. Two contrasting stories will help shed some light on this.

The first is of the rich young ruler in Matthew:

> *[16] Now a man came up to Jesus and asked, "Teacher, what good thing must I do to get eternal life?" [17] "Why do you ask me about what is good?" Jesus replied. "There is only One who is good. If you want to enter life, obey the commandments."*
>
> *[18] "Which ones?" the man inquired. Jesus replied, "Do not murder, do not commit adultery, do not steal, do not give false testimony, [19] honor your father and mother, and love your neighbor as yourself." [20] "All these I have kept," the young man said. "What do I still lack?"*
>
> *[21] Jesus answered, "If you want to be perfect, go, sell your possessions, and give to the poor, and you will have treasure in heaven. Then come, follow me." [22] When the young man heard this, he went away sad, because he had great wealth.*
>
> *[23] Then Jesus said to his disciples, "I tell you the truth, it is hard for a rich man to enter the kingdom of heaven. [24] Again I tell you, it is easier for a camel to go through the eye of a needle than for a rich man to enter the kingdom of God." [25] When the disciples heard this, they were greatly astonished and asked, "Who then can be saved?" [26] Jesus looked at them and said, "With man this is impossible, but with God all things are possible." (Matthew 19: 16-26)*

"faith"

faith is being sure of what we hope for and certain of what we do not see

(Hebrews 11:1)

Jesus responds in an interesting way. He lists only the commandments that have to do with relationships and possessions, (murder, adultery, false witness, theft, honoring your father and mother; and loving your neighbor as yourself) but omits all of the commandments that have to do with God and coveting. The young man informs Jesus that he has kept all of those things but wants to know if there is anything else! This young ruler is standing within an arm's length of Jesus, staring into the eyes of the living God. He is asking for information about eternity but doesn't even understand who he is asking. He calls Him "teacher" because he obviously has not made the connection that Jesus is the Son of God. He thinks He is just another source of information that can bring him the comfort that he wants while still maintaining full control of his life apart from God.

When Christ asked him to sell all that he had and give it to the poor and follow Him, the young man goes away in distress. Christ is not saying that if you have money in the bank you are going to hell! What he is saying to this young man is that money was his God, it

was what was standing between him and dependence on Christ. He is really saying that whatever it is that separates you from God, get rid of it and follow Him.

Jesus is referring to those hurts, habits, and hang-ups that become our gods. Do we love our rage more than our family or God? Do we love our pornography, our desire for control or our addiction more than we love our family and more than we love God? Some people may say, that's not true, I love my family, I love God, but I just can't stop!

We want to assure you that you can decide to start right now and seek a loving, forgiving and caring God. *When you want to love Him more than the garbage in your life, the sins that have separated you from Him will begin to disappear.*

3. Can you in any way identify with the young ruler? If so, how?

_____

_____

_____

_____

_____

In the second story, Luke gives us this account of when Christ was being crucified:

> *³⁹One of the criminals who hung there hurled insults at him: "Aren't you the Christ? Save yourself and us!" ⁴⁰But the other criminal rebuked him. "Don't you fear God," he said, "since you are under the same sentence? ⁴¹We are punished justly, for we are getting what our deeds deserve. But this man has done nothing wrong." ⁴²Then he said, "Jesus, remember me when you come into your kingdom." ⁴³Jesus answered him, "I tell you the truth, today you will be with me in paradise." (Luke 23:39-43)*

The question is, What did that thief hanging on the cross know? Was he educated in the law? Was he looking for the Messiah? Was he a religious person who was diligently obeying the Ten Commandments? On one hand we have the rich young ruler, who knows the law, is often at the temple, keeps the commands out of duty and has a perfect handle on the appearance of religion. He looks good, wants to do better, wants to take pride in his knowledge, but still wants to maintain control of his life and place his own priorities ahead of God. Contrast this with that thief hanging on the cross and his opportunity to seek Christ. So, what did he know?

He had seen a man brutally beaten and nailed to a cross while he was forgiving those doing it. He saw a man praying for guidance, verbally reaching out to his disciples to give them direction and calm them in His hour of darkness. He sees all of this while people mock, insult and curse Jesus. He knows that his own seeking is finished because he sees the actions of Christ, hears His words, and feels the comfort he experiences with Him. In this thief's brokenness, more is revealed to him in a few hours than he could have learned in 50 years of sermons, self-help books and college classes.

That thief was sentenced to death and was a sinner in the eyes of God. He was not in control of what was left of his life and needed salvation. Unlike the rich young ruler, he could see the Son of God with the eyes of someone in brokenness instead of pride. When he asks Jesus to remember him, Christ doesn't tell him about the Ten Commandments, He simply welcomes him home.

4. What can we learn from these stories?

_____
_____
_____
_____
_____

"insanity"
doing the same thing over and over again in the same way while expecting a different result

More questions for reflection

5. Today, am I trusting in myself, in things, and in others or in God and His word?

_____
_____
_____

6. What questions do I still have about God?

_____

_____

_____

_____

7. How can I find the answers to the questions I have in Question 6?

_____

_____

_____

_____

8. Am I reading the Bible simply to gain knowledge or to better understand what God wants me to do with my life?

_____

_____

_____

_____

9. Have you in the past (or present), ever isolated yourself from God or other people?

Journaling Space:

trust

**we made a decision to turn our will and our lives
over to the care of God...**

Read: Psalm 40: 1-17 (He is my help and my deliverer)

trust: noun, verb
(Dictionary): assured reliance on the character, ability, strength, or truth of someone or something
(Faith): Faith in, hope in, confidence in, and dependence upon God alone

In its most basic terms, our pathway to healing can be described as a *decision* followed by a *process*. The decision is made when we admit that our lives have become unmanageable. Then we start our healing process, (usually after reaching some breaking point), when we decide that life is not going to get better by living with the same old fears, habits, and pain. Simply stated, it is when the pain begins to outweigh the benefits of our past behaviors.

Some of us have lived with the pain, the shame, and the guilt of another person's actions for many years. Maybe we have struggled in an abusive or addictive relationship. In some cases, our own wrong thinking led to our own bad choices and sinful behaviors. We turned to things other than God to fill the emptiness in our lives. Maybe we sought peace and fulfillment in substance abuse; or we lived to gain acceptance from other people and value through things. Some of us isolated ourselves, others ate to feel better and still others used work to escape. I (Jim) have had my own struggles with work addiction:

> "When it comes right down to it, I believe my workaholism grew out of a lack of faith in God. I didn't trust Him to meet my needs. For years I felt as if I had to do it all myself. I didn't trust anyone, much less someone I saw as a distant God.
>
> Since an early age, my life had been marked by broken trust. Just before starting high school, I learned I was adopted. Not that there is anything wrong with that in itself, but the timing and how I found out made me feel abandoned by my birth parents and confused by my emotionally distant adoptive ones. I began drifting away from the Lord and walked away from my Catholic upbringing when I was 16 years old. I had no real friends and would deliberately try to avoid anyone who wanted to help me. A series of codependent dating relationships led to an early marriage while I was still in grad school. It ended in divorce just four years later. Even after that I continued to trust only in myself and my own strength. I ran under my own power 100% of the time.

"higher power" a term used in secular recovery in place of God to ensure that any individual, regardless of background can participate in a group and work on their issues

But, during all that insane time, my business career flourished. To avoid the pain of those relationships, I worked nonstop and would become angry with anyone who tried to interfere with my work addiction. I quickly rose through the corporate ranks to highly paid top level executive positions. I had a huge house in an elite neighborhood, a luxury car, and an expensive four-wheel drive truck… all things that I perceived I had earned on my own, through my long hours of labor and hectic travel. I rarely went on vacation, and if I did, I was usually upset that I was away from work and acted out in anger. (Since then, I have realized it wasn't really the money that I was working for, it was my way of trying to fill the deep emptiness inside of me.)

I lived and breathed business. I never really rested, but instead collapsed in exhaustion or illness when too tired to continue. On weekends, I either worked at my job or on a large project around the house. Despite my apparent worldly success, all the relentless working eventually took its toll on my family and business, making me inwardly depressed and outwardly miserable. In my early forties I was divorced a second time. Soon after that, I 'hit the wall' and had a complete emotional, financial, and physical breakdown that led me back to the Lord."

No matter how badly you have acted out in your own life, you too may have been trying to fill a void inside of yourself. But there is always hope. Once we realize that this void exists and that the pain comes from how we try to fill it, we can begin to search for healing.

1. When was the last time you felt a void or emptiness inside yourself? What did you try to do about it?

_____

_____

_____

_____

No matter where you are in the process of healing and recovery, the key to maintaining momentum is trusting in God. It is a lack of trust (or faith) in God that will stop us dead in our tracks. It is a lack of trust in what we know to be true that will derail our spiritual growth. When we trust in Him, we come to believe that God can and will restore us to sanity. When we accept responsibility for our actions and turn our will and our lives over to Jesus Christ, He will fill that void. Only then will we begin to heal completely.

When we rely on ourselves alone to solve our problems, manage relationships, or set our own rules in life, we will always fail. For many of us, this path has led us to such a place of pain that we finally sought out some help. Only then are we able to deal with the "stuff" that stands between us and trusting God's will for our lives. Once we make that decision, it is important that we place our trust in God not reluctantly or halfheartedly, but deliberately and with conviction!

> **²⁷Then he said to Thomas, "Put your finger here; see my hands. Reach out your hand and put it into my side. Stop doubting and believe."**
> **(John 20:27)**

Levels of trust

There are three basic levels of trust. To best explain them, we are going to use an illustration that Christian author and speaker Bruce Wilkinson[1] has used to describe a person's walk of faith. (We have adapted it here to fit our recovery context.) The analogy is built around three chairs.

Chair One

In Chair One we have people who are committed to a worldview that holds the planets rotate around the sun, the sun rotates within the galaxy and the galaxy rotates around them. They have bumper stickers on their vehicles that read, "HE WHO DIES WITH THE MOST TOYS WINS". They are committed to playing, eating, partying, and doing anything that makes them feel good or appeals to their sense of self-fulfillment. They do not donate time or money to causes. They like Christmas and Easter only because both are paid holidays. This chair is the place that those of us that have histories of addictive or compulsive behavior can relate to. We used to live and lived to use, or in the case of a person with a compulsive behavior, we lived to manage and managed to live. We acted out in whatever way we felt appropriate at the time; we shrugged off the consequences for our actions and returned immediately and without delay to our old behaviors when we could. If anyone approached us or attempted to intervene, we would lash out at them and/or separate ourselves from them. We were in total control of our lives and didn't need anyone's help, least of all God's, to get through the day. Life's top priority is self, everyone, and everything else is a distant second and God isn't even on the list.

"enable"
to assist people in continuing with their self-destructive behavior

Chair Two

The Second Chair is occupied by people who are caught in a struggle between their concept of God and their desire to do as they please. The vast majority of people in our world sit in this chair. They consider themselves to be good people, but they are usually burdened with guilt and anxiety as they struggle with either recognizing God or continuing to act out. They go to church when it is convenient, unless a bigger priority comes up. They pray only in crisis. They own a Bible but do not read it. They have a connection to the Christian life only because that is how they were raised.

This is the place where most of us are when we begin to question our habits and lifestyles. We sense something isn't right, but we don't know how to find the answers. People try to tell us that we are messing up our lives and we know deep down inside that they are right. We rely mostly on self-help, willpower and other people, places, and things to make us happy. Our priorities are based on the need of the moment.

[1] www.brucewilkinson.com

For example, today the sudden illness of a child may cause us to reach out to God for healing, but tomorrow's flat tire becomes the wrath of a vengeful God who is bent on destroying our life. Today, going to church is imperative, next week we miss because one of the kids has a soccer game. Second chair people say one thing and do another. They talk about what is important in their life but they act differently. They are not anchored to any conviction or absolute truth. *Second Chair people often raise First Chair children.* Children watch the lives of their parents and realize at a young age that God is not important enough to make a priority and they reject Him at an early age.

Chair Three

In the Third Chair are people who are deeply committed to trusting in God. They consider a relationship with Him their number one priority. They make life decisions based on His Word. They place their relationship with God ahead of their spouse, family, children, and work. They are deeply devoted to serving others and actively look for opportunities to do so. They are guided by the concept of stewardship rather than guilt. They give of their time, talent, and treasure because they recognize that these are gifts from God, and not things that they have earned themselves. They own a Bible and read it regularly to answer the questions of life. They trust that God has a good and perfect plan and that He can make all things work for good for those that place their faith in Him. In the church body, these are the people who are in service positions, who sponsor, who lead groups and who come early and set up chairs. They know that the only way to continue to grow in their healing and recovery is to give away what has been freely given to them.

The one thing that separates these three chairs is *trust*.

- In Chair One we trust in ourselves
- In Chair Two we do not know who or what to trust
- In Chair Three we trust in Christ

2. What chair are you in today? Why?

_____
_____
_____
_____
_____

Biblical reference

How can we apply this idea to our lives? We can all relate to being in any one of these chairs at different points in our life, but how can we move to Chair Three? God's word gives us clear direction as we attempt to understand this idea:

> *[1]Therefore, I urge you, brothers, in view of God's mercy, to offer your bodies as living sacrifices, holy and pleasing to God—this is your spiritual act of worship. (Romans 12:1)*

Paul is not asking us to offer our talent, our encouragement, or our best intentions to God. He is asking us to offer our bodies and everything that we are comprised of. He is urging us to come to God with all that we have. Paul is advising us to place all of our time, talent, and treasure under His care, and allow God to be in total control of our will and lives.

Most of us have compartmentalized relationships with God. We are willing to give Him an hour on Sunday morning, but the rest of the week is ours for business as usual. We know that He has given us all that we have, but we won't trust Him with our finances. We reject His principles for running our relationships, home, and families.

3. What are the areas of your life that you have withheld from God? Are you withholding any right now?

_____

_____

_____

_____

_____

"safe person"
someone that can be trusted with the depth of our personal truth and brokenness because of an understanding of their own. an unsafe person would be the exact opposite

To truly heal and to grow in this world we need to be rooted in something bigger than ourselves. Christ assures us of this as follows:

> *[46]I have come into the world as a light, so that no one who believes in me should stay in darkness. (John 12:46)*

We see the effects of lack of relationship with God all around us like marriages that fail when the kids leave home; men who die within months of retiring from long careers; people unable to overcome addictions, all because they do not climb out of denial and find something larger than themselves. If pleasing oneself is the highest goal we have in life, there will come a day when the party will end. The noise will stop, the endless distractions will cease to amuse us and we'll be forced to confront the emptiness of our lives. There is an entire book of the Bible, (Ecclesiastes, written by Solomon) that is dedicated to the subject. True peace, healing and recovery come only in Chair Three.

Even the most dedicated secularists in Alcoholics Anonymous often believe they need to trust in a higher power to succeed in recovery. But how should we define that higher power? We do it by deciding what that power needs to be in our lives. We need a God who is loving and caring, who is able to see the past and the future and loves us unconditionally anyway. We need a God who offers such love to us along with forgiveness.

If you can find omnipotent power, unconditional love and grace in another person, place, or thing we are anxious to speak with you about your discovery. In all our years of searching, we have found only one place where we could find the strength needed for complete healing. It is in the person of Jesus. Not because it is a religion… *but because it is not.* A relationship with Jesus is not a religious thing. It is a personal relationship, based on our personal understanding and desire to turn our will and our life over to Christ. All we need to do is trust in Him.

> [16]*For God so loved the world that he gave his one and only Son, that whoever believes in him shall not perish but have eternal life. (John 3:16)*

Famous preacher D.L. Moody did a revival meeting the night before the Great Chicago Fire of 1871. That particular evening, he did not give people a chance to respond to the message to accept Christ. It was reported the next day that of the hundreds of people who were there that night, many perished in the flames. Moody never again stood up to talk about God without asking people to make a decision for Christ.

If we ask WHEN we need to trust in Him, the answer is a clear and resounding NOW! If we have already made the decision to turn our will and our lives over to the care of God, then we need to be sure that we did it without reservation. We need to be sure that there are no areas of our will or our lives that we've held back. Not our time, our guilt, our anger, our self-centeredness, our addictions, our lust, or our desire to control others. No matter what it is, we need to stop carrying the weight of it and give it to Christ.

Devotional Verse

⁴ The Sovereign LORD has given me an instructed tongue,
 to know the word that sustains the weary.
 He wakens me morning by morning,
 wakens my ear to listen like one being taught.
⁵ The Sovereign LORD has opened my ears,
 and I have not been rebellious;
 I have not drawn back.
⁶ I offered my back to those who beat me,
 my cheeks to those who pulled out my beard;
 I did not hide my face
 from mocking and spitting.
⁷ Because the Sovereign LORD helps me;
 I will not be disgraced.
 Therefore, I have set my face like flint,
 and I know I will not be put to shame.
⁸ He who vindicates me is near.
 Who then will bring charges against me?
 Let us face each other!
 Who is my accuser?
 Let him confront me!
⁹ It is the Sovereign LORD who helps me.
 Who is he that will condemn me?
 They will all wear out like a garment;
 the moths will eat them up.
¹⁰ Who among you fears the LORD
 and obeys the word of his servant?
 Let him who walks in the dark,
 who has no light,
 trust in the name of the LORD
 and rely on his God.
¹¹ But now, all you who light fires
 and provide yourselves with flaming torches,
 go, walk in the light of your fires
 and of the torches you have set ablaze.
 This is what you shall receive from my hand:
 You will lie down in torment.
            (Isaiah 50:4-11)

More questions for reflection

4. Who or what else are you trusting in today other than God?

_____

_____

_____

_____

5. What is it that stops you from fully trusting God?

_____

_____

_____

_____

6. What things in your past confuse you about the true nature of God?

_____

_____

_____

_____

7. What personal testimony do you have about God's faithfulness during the trials you've experienced in life? Would you consider sharing it with others?

8. Have you turned your will and your life over to God? If so, how, and when? If not, why not?

Journaling Space:

fearless

making a searching and fearless moral inventory of ourselves...

Read: Psalm 27:1 (The Lord is my light and my salvation)

Fear·less: adjective
(Dictionary): free from fear
(Faith): trusting and respecting God

We have only two choices in life

If given a choice (and we are), which would you choose? To lead a life controlled by fear, guilt, and shame; or one in which you faced your past, fears, and doubts to live in victory? There is no third option. If we want to live a fearless life, the opportunity is clearly open to each and every one of us. *All we need to do is make that choice.*

Certainly, no one wants to live in a world controlled by the person who injured us, the things that we did when we abused alcohol or the codependent things that we should have never done. We don't have to if we accept Christ as the pathway to living a fearless life. It is the reality of who we are in Him that can truly begin to heal our lives.

In light of the huge change that we can achieve in overcoming this fear, it is amazing how so many people stall here and cannot seem to close the door on their past. That's because when we leave a bad marriage; recognize a pattern in our lives that we don't want to repeat; or simply stop acting out, we have changed our environment, or our response to it, but we have done little to change ourselves. It's like the person who stops drinking alcohol, but still acts out as if they did drink.

It is God's greatest desire that we live life to the fullest and achieve the great joy that He has planned for us. To us, our present circumstances may seem overwhelming, pointless, and filled with pain, but God is capable of viewing our situation from an eternal perspective. He assures us that if we place our trust in Him, even the most painful of those losses will be made whole. He offers us hope.

What prevents us from doing this?

Simply put, fear of change, fear of the past and fear of failing. What causes these fears? Fear is nothing more than a lack of faith in God. Fear is often a trigger that fuels our anger.

"acting out"
continuing in or relapsing to destructive behaviors like raging, abusing, gambling, enabling, gossiping, or drinking because of unresolved issues in our lives

it is what stops us from overcoming the things we should conquer in our lives. Fear stops us from seizing opportunities. Fear will destroy our growth and healing. Fear is a tool of satan.

In faith, there is no fear that cannot be overcome. Christ came to help us get a glimpse of what the Kingdom of Heaven is like and to show us the kind of victorious life that God wants us to live. In His Sermon on the Mount, Jesus says "Don't be afraid!" Christ will give you direction and supply your needs. Here, He gives us a formula that will allow us to live a life without fear:

> *^{25}"Therefore, I tell you, do not worry about your life, what you will eat or drink; or about your body, what you will wear. Is not life more important than food, and the body more important than clothes? ^{26}Look at the birds of the air; they do not sow or reap or store away in barns, and yet your heavenly Father feeds them. Are you not much more valuable than they? ^{27}Who of you by worrying can add a single hour to his life?*
> *^{28}"And why do you worry about clothes? See how the lilies of the field grow. They do not labor or spin. ^{29}Yet I tell you that not even Solomon in all his splendor was dressed like one of these. ^{30}If that is how God clothes the grass of the field, which is here today and tomorrow is thrown into the fire, will he not much more clothe you, O you of little faith? ^{31}So do not worry, saying, 'What shall we eat?' or 'What shall we drink?' or 'What shall we wear?' ^{32}For the pagans run after all these things, and your heavenly Father knows that you need them. ^{33} But seek first His kingdom and His righteousness, and all these things will be given to you as well. ^{34} Therefore do not worry about tomorrow, for tomorrow will worry about itself. Each day has enough trouble of its own."*
> *(Matthew 6:33-34)*

Here is what Jesus is saying will be added to you in this verse...where you will live, what you will eat, what you will drink and what you will wear. Christ is asking us not to be filled with fear, but to instead be filled with faith in all things large and small, and then follow Him.

1. Are you ever afraid of God turning His back on you? If so why?

_____

_____

_____

Are you fearless?

In doing this, we are being asked to do something that may be totally foreign to us. It requires us to make a moral inventory and in doing so to be *fearless* about it. To take such an inventory we must examine our lives in the hard light of day without excuse and then face the truth we discover. We live in a culture that is guided by fear. Many of us live lives that are ruled by persistent and painful fear. Psychologists tell us that the vast majority of modern-day decisions are made, not in terms of moral values, but because of fear of loss. We make changes to our lifestyles when we have a heart attack because we are scared of dying. We hide in guilt and shame in relationships because we are fearful that speaking the truth will cause conflict. We stay in jobs that we hate because we are afraid of change.

We can truly be fearless if we "FEAR" God

Understanding the fear of God is a remarkable and important cornerstone of Christian healing. We may have grown up being taught that God was angry, that He would destroy us or visit incredible hardships on us if we did not listen and obey. We may have grown up with an angry father (or stepfather) or been the victim of some abuse by someone in a position of authority. Most of us can say that we have been rebellious, wanting things our own way. We may have fought against anything that we believed was painting us into a corner. All of these kinds of misconceptions lead us to a misunderstanding about the fear of God. If we are going to lead fearless lives as believers, the only thing that we can fear is the One who gives us the power and confidence to be fearless. So how can we reconcile this? How can we be in love with anyone that we are being asked to be afraid of?

Let's put this idea through an important biblical filter. Some call it the filter of love; others refer to it as the Holy Spirit. It is this interaction with the power of pure and living love that allows the Bible to be a truly living and perfect book. If we take a passage like Leviticus 19:11-18 and use the word *love* to replace the word *fear* we start to get a better understanding of what kind of fear we are being asked to embrace in order to seek a relationship with God. He is pure and steadfast love, but before Him the mountains melt like wax. He will not abandon us or forsake us, but separated from Him we live an eternity of suffering and pain. Look at this passage and use fear and love interchangeably.

> *¹¹"Do not steal." Do not cheat one another. "Do not lie. ¹²"Do not use my name to swear a falsehood and so profane the name of your God. I am the LORD. ¹³"Do not cheat or rob anyone. "Always pay your hired workers promptly. ¹⁴"Show your (love) fear of God by treating the deaf with respect and by not taking advantage of the blind. I am the LORD.*
> *¹⁵"Always judge your neighbors fairly, neither favoring the poor nor showing deference to the rich. ¹⁶"Do not spread slanderous gossip among your people. "Do not try to get ahead at the cost of your neighbor's life, for I am the LORD. ¹⁷"Do not nurse hatred in your heart for any of your relatives. "Confront your neighbors directly so you will not be held guilty for their crimes. ¹⁸"Never seek revenge or bear a grudge against anyone but love your neighbor as yourself. I am the LORD. (Lev. 19:11-18)*

Within this context we are not simply talking about respect although it is part of the point. We are talking about a pure love, love so important to us that we would be devastated or, "afraid" of it being withdrawn from us. When we can be awed by the power of God, swept up by the overwhelming power of His love, His greatness, His glory, and His strength, then

"boundaries"

the setting of healthy rules of engagement between you and the people around you at work, home, church, and family we are in a place where He can begin to teach us.

Fearing God means living like we understand His awesome power. He is big enough to wipe away the sin and regret of yesterday. He is big enough to handle our trials of today. He has tomorrow in the palm of His hand. Through His Son, He has changed us forever and we cannot be separated from Him. We can have the power that created the universe in the very center of our lives by beginning a relationship with Him.

A roadmap for our recovery

Many of us, some for the first time, need to face our issues and sin without excuses. A former member of one of my small groups told the following story about something he did before he entered recovery:

> "I was responsible for stealing money donated to the Cancer Society at my grandmother's funeral. I used the cash to buy drugs. I spent the next 6 years suffering the pain of the guilt that I carried because of it. I tried to justify it by saying to myself… She was dead and the money was of no value to her; she died of cancer, so what good did the Cancer Society do for her? What I needed to do instead was to admit to it for what it was… something I had done wrong."

We can't deal with the emotional pain in our lives unless we look at things for what they really are. We can't deal with the loss of a marriage unless we look at what role we ourselves took in its failure. We can't recover from substance abuse issues unless we determine why we placed ourselves in jeopardy in the first place. In some cases, we will find that it was just a mistake of youth or clouded judgment based on appearances. Some of us will discover that we married a carbon copy of our controlling and abusive mother, or our angry and addicted father in an effort to deal with the past in our own destructive way. Very few of us are in damaging relationships that don't feed things inside of us that need to be dealt with. We can't deal with these types of things unless we place our actions in the hard light of day without excuse.

> **[40] Let us examine our ways and test them, and let us return to the LORD (Lamentations 3:40)**

2. What are those things in your life that you are still making excuses for? (Or blaming others for?)

_____

_____

_____

_____

When we get to this point, we need a roadmap to share with God and another person so that we can be assured that we are truly forgiven. When we deal with our own failures as part of our healing, we will need to have a clear view of what those are (without excuse) so we can ask God to remove them. We need to come to grips with the fact that we do not use, we do not explode, we do not manipulate, transgress, or sin because of anything that any other person does to us. We act out because we want to, because we choose to and because that is how we have always chosen to deal with things.

Biblical reference

To learn how lives can be changed by trusting God, an excellent place to look is in the book of Acts. Picking up the story, we find the disciples living in fear after the death of Christ. They had scattered, denied Jesus, and hid. But after the resurrection, a change occurred that launched the early church. It turned their panic and doubt into fearless power. So great was the change that they went out directly to those who crucified Jesus and fearlessly began to preach the gospel. Such change came the very moment they accepted the help of God though the power of the Holy Spirit and their lives changed forever.

> *²⁴But God raised him from the dead, freeing him from the agony of death, because it was impossible for death to keep its hold on him. ²⁵David said about him: "I saw the Lord always before me. Because he is at my right hand, I will not be shaken. ²⁶Therefore my heart is glad and my tongue rejoices; my body also will live in hope, ²⁷because you will not abandon me to the grave, nor will you let your Holy One see decay. ²⁸You have made known to me the paths of life; you will fill me with joy in your presence."*
>
> *²⁹"Brothers, I can tell you confidently that the patriarch David died and was buried, and his tomb is here to this day. ³⁰But he was a prophet and knew that God had promised him on oath that he would place one of his descendants on his throne. ³¹Seeing what was ahead, he spoke of the resurrection of the Christ, that he was not abandoned to the grave, nor did his body see decay. ³²God has raised this Jesus to life, and we are all witnesses of the fact.*
>
> *³³Exalted to the right hand of God, he has received from the Father the promised Holy Spirit and has poured out what you now see and hear. ³⁴For David did not ascend to heaven, and yet he said, The Lord said to my Lord: Sit at my right hand ³⁵until I make your enemies a footstool for your feet."*
>
> *³⁶"Therefore, let all Israel be assured of this: God has made this Jesus, whom you crucified, both Lord and Christ." ³⁷When the people heard this, they were cut to the heart and said to Peter and the other apostles, "Brothers, what shall we do?" ³⁸Peter replied, "Repent and be baptized,*

"secrets"

those things that we hold on to in our walk of faith out of shame and guilt

every one of you, in the name of Jesus Christ for the forgiveness of your sins. And you will receive the gift of the Holy Spirit. [39] The promise is for you and your children and for all who are far off—for all whom the Lord our God will call." [40] With many other words he warned them; and he pleaded with them, "Save yourselves from this corrupt generation." [41] Those who accepted his message were baptized, and about three thousand were added to their number that day. (Acts 2:37-41)

When the risen Lord began to work in their lives, the disciples finally understood what He had been trying to tell them all along. If we live to glorify God, He will use us in powerful and unimaginable ways. If we live lives in relationship with Him, honestly facing our past, we can defeat fear with faith. Nothing is too dirty to be cleaned, nothing too dark to be illuminated and no injury is too deep for Christ to help us heal. When we live fearless lives, nothing on this earth can separate us from Him.

Questions for reflection

3. What areas of my life are still controlled by fear or by my past?

_____

_____

_____

_____

_____

4. What are those things in my life that I need to face without excuse?

_____

_____

_____

_____

5. List the top two or three things that you would like to put behind you.

_____

_____

_____

_____

6. List the healthy things that God is doing in your life that you wish that you had more of.

_____

_____

_____

_____

_____

7. List one or more persons in your circle of faith who you can trust that you can share your lists with.

_____

_____

_____

When we share the pain of our past, seek God's forgiveness and trust in His grace, our lives will be changed forever.

Getting help with your fearless inventory:

Things to leave behind: Galations 5: 19-21

Things to carry forward: Galations 5: 22-25

Journaling Space:

forgiven

we openly examine and confess our faults to God and to someone of faith who has earned our trust...

Read: Romans 3:19 (We all need forgiveness)

for·given: adjective
(Dictionary): pardoned; to be excused for an offense
(Faith): to be completely and totally absolved by God's grace from payment for our sins

The concept of forgiveness is at the very center of Christianity. It is one thing that truly differentiates our faith from other religious ideas. Forgiveness is the message of the cross. If we reject the suffering and death of Jesus that guaranteed forgiveness, then we reject God Himself. If we accept it, we can put our old life behind us and enter into a new one defined by peace and promise. If we don't want to be free of our sin, our pain, and our mistakes, then we have missed the point of the relationship that God wants to have with us.

Anyone who has experienced difficulty with organized religion will recognize the problem that Christians face if they believe that they don't have things in their past or present that need to be forgiven. This can make churches very unfriendly places, especially for people experiencing real pain in their lives. When those of us who make up the church body are more interested in appearing sinless than we are in openly discussing those things we need forgiveness for, we miss the point of a relationship with Christ and His sacrifice for us. When that is the case, our hope of healing is stolen from us by "religion". Christ worked hard in his brief time with us to set us free from the lies of the world and the weight of man-made religion.

Religion (as opposed to a relationship with Christ), gives us a set of rules constructed to create the illusion of being able to measure up. Religion tells us that if we follow the rules in just the right way, we can please God and earn back our forgiveness. This has been the cornerstone of every man-made religion that the world has ever known. The problem comes when we look to other humans to help us figure out when we have done enough to please God.

On the other hand, the world tells us to get over the things of the past, to forget about them, or to blame them on the failure of our parents and others who have "done us wrong". We can pretend to have forgotten, but the pain, the shame and the guilt will linger. We can blame those around us, turn to destructive behaviors, or try to find someone else to fix it, *but we will only heal when we accept God's forgiveness*. His forgiveness is available to all of us, no matter what we have done. There is nothing so terrible that He will not forgive

"adult child"
refers to a person who was parented in a home that was affected by alcoholism, substance abuse or other serious dysfunction

us if we will only ask. However, that doesn't mean that we are necessarily free of the earthly consequences of those actions. We may have trials as a result of bad choices. These are not punishments; such trials are *consequences.* (You might punish a child for repeatedly trying to touch a hot stove but is not punishment to be burned by it.)

It is only in admitting our need to be forgiven and in being "broken before God" that we can begin to find a place of peace. His forgiveness happens in the very moment we accept His assurance for the future. Jesus came to comfort those of us who are tired of looking to religion or the world for answers. He knew that if we were tired of failing, of fighting, of measuring up and of trying to fix ourselves, His message would find a receptive heart.

It is impossible to move ahead in recovery or in our journey of faith without truly understanding the power of forgiveness. This has powerful meaning in the Christian community because our "higher power" is a God who allows us to work on our issues (or our salvation). The God we need to come to understand is all-knowing, long-suffering, capable of performing miracles and more than powerful enough to forgive us our sins. Seeing God in this way helps us understand that we ourselves do not have the power needed to change our own lives, to forgive ourselves or even to truly forgive or to change someone else.

It is in our human desire to take our power back, to avoid dealing with God, to isolate ourselves, to keep our issues secret or to find a place where we can look good and fit in. This is a pathway to failure. Anytime we are trying to find our way to forgiveness under our own steam, we are working in the power of idolatry verses seeking the power of relationship with God. True forgiveness is something that we get through God's power, not from our own. He not only wants to forgive us, but in doing so wants to restore us and create within us a power of brokenness.

We see in the book of Luke a remarkable example of Christ's frustration with religious people. These were people who didn't want to understand or admit their own weaknesses or failures. In the story, Jesus was invited to a dinner at the home of a Pharisee. While there, a woman of notorious reputation approaches Him. She washed his feet with oil and her tears, and then dried them with her hair. The Pharisees, (the "enlightened" religious types of the day) were appalled not just at the woman for her shameful display and interruption, but at Christ for even allowing the woman to come close to Him.

> *[39]When the Pharisee who had invited him saw this, he said to himself, "If this man were a prophet, he would know who is touching him and what kind of woman she is—that she is a sinner." (Luke 7:39)*

The Pharisees (self-appointed representatives of God) didn't even want the woman near them. Why? They had convinced themselves that they were already perfect in the eyes of God and that the sins of others were something that they needed to recognize and condemn. Because of that, they had rendered themselves useless in doing the very thing that God expects each of us to do. He expects us to reach out to the hurting, the sick and the lost. They wrongly thought they had worked their way into a position equal to God. They wrongly believed that they did the right things, dressed the right way, and ate the right food. In their distorted view, this woman would have to do the same to be acceptable.

What we have here is a sad analogy of much of the modern church. It is at the point when we begin to think we have all the answers and that we have our lives together that religion and legalism creep into our lives. Legalism will destroy our spiritual growth and ability to lead others to Christ. We can become recovery legalists who point fingers as easily as we can become religious legalists who defend those things that make us comfortable in church to the exclusion of those literally dying to hear the good news of God's forgiveness. Only when we are in a place of grateful and humble recognition of forgiveness ourselves, can we effectively share God's message of forgiveness with others.

We have people all around us in churches who cling to the idea that they have been forgiven of very little and that people who are in need of forgiveness are not worthy to be in their midst. They have convinced themselves that they are good people, doing good things and becoming closer to God through their own actions. But, when they come into contact with someone who is consumed with grief; struggling with an eating disorder; fighting with authority figures; sporting green hair and body piercings; an addict; someone struggling with divorce, pornography, anger, or just everyday life, they immediately become very uncomfortable. The truth of the matter is since they tend to see all of those things as "bad" and because they see themselves as "good", they attempt to immediately distance themselves from "those people, with those problems". *This type of thinking is not in keeping with God's desire to reach every one of us*. This is especially true when we recognize that we have all fallen short ourselves.

Since the fall of Adam and Eve, no one, no matter how "good" we think we are, can stand before a perfect God and defend our actions, thoughts, and deeds. To God, sin is sin. The deacon at a church who won't allow a convicted sex offender to attend a service is in a greater place of offence with God than the person he seeks to keep out of church. This is because he stands in total conflict with the message of Christ and the movement of the Holy Spirit within a lost child of God who wants to be loved inside a community of believers.

God knows something about forgiveness that seems to escape most people. He didn't allow His Son to be crucified to cover only selected sins. He did it for all of us and for all of our sins, not just the big ones. He has enough forgiveness in Him to forgive both murderers and hypocrites at the same time.

When we admit the mess we have created in our lives and look to Him for forgiveness, something incredible happens. Our lives change. We become filled with a joy and peace that's bigger than our money problems, the abusive actions of our past and our shame and our guilt. It is a joy and a peace that can go beyond all that we could have ever imagined. However, there is a catch to this. We need to admit to our unworthiness in order to be worthy of forgiveness. We need to see the futility of our own works and accept His free gift of forgiveness. Only when we receive this gift in brokenness can we begin a new life built on God's love. And it is only when we accept God's forgiveness that we can start to see the pain of others as worthy of our forgiveness, our attention, our prayer, and our actions. When Christ was teaching the Pharisees about the sin of the woman He told them this:

"one day at a time"

the realization that yesterday cannot be changed nor can tomorrow be guaranteed... we live today as though it was our last

> *⁴⁷"Therefore, I tell you, her many sins have been forgiven—for she loved much. But he who has been forgiven little loves little." ⁴⁸Then Jesus said to her, "Your sins are forgiven." ⁴⁹The other guests began to say among themselves, "Who is this who even forgives sins?" ⁵⁰Jesus said to the woman, "Your faith has saved you; go in peace." (Luke 7:47-50)*

1. Since you woke up this morning, what things have been in your heart, your words or your actions that might require God's forgiveness? (No superficial answers.)

_____

_____

_____

_____

Further understanding forgiveness

To heal, we must separate ourselves from our past as we can legitimately recall. Then we become people living in the strength of Christ. To do this, we simply need to pull all our junk out of the closet of our lives and look at it in the hard light of day. We need to see what still fits with who we are in our walk of faith and what doesn't. If we fail to look at our past, our mistakes, our pain, and our weaknesses, we are rejecting a clear opportunity to embrace and live in God's forgiveness. All this does is leave us living in the painful messes that we've created for ourselves. If we can see all sin as equal in the eyes of God, then we can stop hating those we need to forgive and begin forgiving ourselves in a new way.

If we can come to grips with the fact that all of humanity suffers with the disease of sin, then we have gained some ground. When we understand that everyone has sinned and fallen short of the perfection of God, then admitting our sin to others becomes easier.

There is one more barrier that we may have to overcome to complete this task. Doubt often stands between us and achieving true forgiveness. Here are two passages of scripture that can help us to overcome doubt and come to an understanding of God's forgiveness.

> *²²Jesus answered and said to them, "Go and tell John the things you have seen and heard that the blind see, the lame walk, the lepers are cleansed, the deaf hear, the dead are raised, the poor have the gospel preached to them. (Luke 7:22)*

When we take this comment that Christ makes to the disciples of John the Baptist and place it in context with other scripture, the messages recorded in the gospels show us that we can overcome doubt by recognizing what God is doing in our lives and the lives of those around us. Consider this from Matthew:

> *¹Jesus stepped into a boat, crossed over and came to his own town. ²Some men brought to him a paralytic, lying on a mat. When Jesus saw their faith, he said to the paralytic, "Take heart, son; your sins are forgiven." ³At this, some of the teachers of the law said to themselves, "This fellow is blaspheming!" ⁴Knowing their thoughts, Jesus said, "Why do you entertain evil thoughts in your hearts? ⁵Which is easier: to say, 'Your sins are forgiven,' or to say, 'Get up and walk'? ⁶But so that you may know that the Son of Man has authority on earth to forgive sins. .. " Then he said to the paralytic, "Get up, take your mat and go home." ⁷And the man got up and went home. ⁸When the crowd saw this, they were filled with awe; and they praised God, who had given such authority to men.*
> *(Matthew 9:1-8)*

Do you believe in the power of Jesus Christ to forgive sin? Jesus wants us to make a decision about this. Many of us go through our lives doubting that we can ever be forgiven. Unfortunately, we are often surrounded by others who also doubt. If we allow them to, they can and will discourage us.

In Matthew 9 above, Christ sees the hearts of those religious types who don't believe and doubt His ability to forgive sin. Christ asks them the same question that we need to ask ourselves as we make an attempt to grow in our faith. "Why are you thinking evil in your hearts?" He is asking them why they are choosing darkness over light when they have a clear decision to make. They would have just come from the temple, dressed just right and having read their scripture for the day. But their hearts were filled with anger and disbelief. Here Jesus isn't saying that doubt itself is evil. He simply sees that their hearts were not right with God. He also sees that they have no desire to see God in any other way than the one that they already understood. Christ's response here addresses doubt in a practical way. If we doubt the authority of Christ to do miracles in people's lives, then we will doubt His authority to forgive sin.

If we have any doubt in our hearts about God's ability to change lives we need to look around. If we look with a heart that seeks healing and forgiveness, we will see the miracles of changed lives at every turn.

When we acknowledge that lives are being changed in the name of Christ, we can know that Christ is who He claims to be. He can change lives. He can and will forgive your sins, no matter how terrible. To prove this to ourselves, we need only look to people who have been though Christ-centered healing or recovery and ask them. What you will hear from them will be evidence of His ability to heal and forgive those around us.

"isolate"

to run away from or intentionally avoid contact with those who can support you in your journey of faith

2. Is there anything in your life that you fear is too big to be forgiven by God?

_____

_____

_____

_____

_____

3. What have you left off of your answer to Question 2 that you don't want others to know?

_____

_____

_____

_____

_____

Giving and receiving help

The way to healing, forgiveness and faith is found in the company of others. Christ sees not just the faith of the paralytic man, but those people who are with him. Seeing their faith, Jesus said to the man, "Take courage, son. Your sins are forgiven." This paralytic could not have come to Christ by himself. On the other hand, satan wants us to be alone; he wants us consumed with anger; isolated by fear and doubt; separated from others in bitterness or depression or simply isolated in the secrets that we fear others will come to know. *The evil one wants us to doubt that Christ can forgive us.*

In the language of healing, forgiveness comes in the company of others. We don't keep our inventory to ourselves but share it with God and another person. There is good news for you; two out of the three guests coming to the party already know the truth, you, and God!

the people around us. The person or persons who you share your inventory with in a safe small group setting will also become part of your healing. Your confidence will give them a clearer understanding of the power of God to heal and forgive. Christ tells us that there is power in company when we meet in His name and He promises to show up!

> *[19]"Again, I tell you that if two of you on earth agree about anything you ask for, it will be done for you by my Father in heaven. [20]For where two or three come together in my name, there am I with them."*
> *(Matthew 18:20)*

Don't run away from accountability and companionship at this place in your life. The answer to the peace that you are seeking is found when you combine your faith in Christ with a community of believers.

Asking for God's forgiveness with confidence

When we face the issues of our past and our sin openly and transparently, we can do it with a confidence that may be hard to grasp for those who do not understand true Christianity. Our confidence comes from our understanding of the great lengths, pain and suffer- ing that God has personally undertaken to bring us to a place where we can meet with others who share our faith to find true assurance of forgiveness.

> *[16]For God so loved the world that he gave his one and only Son, that whoever believes in him shall not perish but have eternal life. [17]For God did not send his Son into the world to condemn the world, but to save the world through him. [18]Whoever believes in him is not condemned, but whoever does not believe stands condemned already because he has not believed in the name of God's one and only Son. (John 3:16-18)*

Secular recovery groups tell us that we can create any higher power that makes us feel good. But for true forgiveness, we must confess our sins to the one true God… not simply to another person, spirit, or thing. If we will choose to confess our sins and repent, then trusting in Him and His ability to forgive, we will finally be separated from our past. There is no time and place like right now to seek and accept the forgiveness of God.

God is ready to forgive, and if you are a believer in Christ and willing to turn from your sinful past, He already has. That's all we need to do know to confirm our faith and begin a new level of relationship with God.

"attitude of gratitude"

a lifestyle built on recognizing the power and the blessings that God gives us in the midst of life's trials

Sharing with one another

Once we have confessed our sins to God, there is still much to be gained by sharing our struggles and shortcomings with others. It brings us into a stronger and more authentic community with each other. It allows us to reject guilt and shame and it opens the door to a new and more powerful ministry than we could ever have imagined. This move to transparency will not come unless we confidently share our issues in the safety of a Christ-centered community of faith, healing, and recovery. When you seek out someone to share with, make sure that they have a working knowledge of this process. That way there can be no confusion about what you are hoping to accomplish.

Gaining the assurance of God's forgiveness and fearlessly sharing your issues with others will be a life changing event for you. How can you share the good news of a changed life, a changed marriage, escape from the pain of codependency or ending addiction if you are unsure that you have been forgiven for such things yourself? Christ wants us to speak to one another with confidence without shame and guilt. satan wants to keep us silent!

Another former small group member related this story recently:

> "In my case, this sharing with others took place in a parish hall in Prince Albert, Saskatchewan on one Christmas Eve. My sponsor had driven me across the frozen December landscape of a Canadian winter to sit with an Anglican priest.
>
> It was something that I was not looking forward to. I had no idea what an Anglican priest was like, except for sitting through an Anglican Christmas service when I was 14 years old. I had a special dislike for organized religion and was prepared for something more like a trip to the dentist. My sponsor had recommended this approach, primarily because of my deep mistrust of organized religion. I had been experiencing difficulties in knowing exactly what a "higher power" meant and the notion of obtaining divine forgiveness in this way was difficult for me to understand.
>
> But it was apparent to me by the end of the meeting that the things of my past, however evil and dark they seemed to me, had little impact on this man of the cloth. He was far more interested in my current state of belief and my plans for turning away from my past behaviors than he was in the details of my indiscretions. He had a truly Christian perspective that was, to my way of thinking, quite unique. His comments on forgiveness were based on me making room for God in the very center of my life. After a review of my inventory, he circled the words "self-

centered behavior" ... meaning I hadn't allowed something else besides *me* into the center of my being. It is what I now call 'making room for God.' It was what I thought I had done before. I had a deep conviction and desire to talk about a changed life and to let Him lead me. However, it was in coming this far that I began to see the broader effects of my choice. I had been offered a kingdom; eternal life; a relationship; a community; and a new, better way of life. All I needed to do to pass through this door was to understand that a promise of a relationship with the living God had been offered to me. The experience left me with a deep appreciation for this process. To be successful in this effort to leave my past behind I needed to remake my center. I needed to build a place for God to come and live in me. More importantly, I needed to know that once I prepared the space, God would live within me!"

Small groups of true believers, even if it's just two or three people, can often be a powerful place to heal. They provide an opportunity to turn our problems, our disbelief, our fears, our doubts, our shame, and our guilt into the ministry that God wants us to have. Such groups allow us to reach out and embrace people who hurt as much (or more) than we do, but who have not yet found the answer. When someone in your small group hears you share your story along with your experience, strength, and hope, you minister to them. God designed us to heal in the company of others while joined together in our faith in Him.

(This is why we do not try to "fix" one another in one-on-one or in small groups. When we tell someone publicly that they "should do this or fix that" we are passing judgment on them for their past or current actions.)

Jesus Christ alone has the ability to change our hearts and our lives. Don't be afraid to confidently ask Him to come into the center of your being!

Biblical reference

In chapter eight of the book of John we get an incredible opportunity to see forgiveness through God's eyes. The story begins when righteous people from the temple, teachers of the law and Pharisees are planning to stone a woman who has been caught in the act of adultery. They brought her to Christ, and being students of the law, they sought to either lure Jesus into conspiring with them or cause Him to refute the law.

> *[4]... and said to Jesus, "Teacher, this woman was caught in the act of adultery. [5]In the Law Moses commanded us to stone such women. Now what do you say?" [6]They were using this question as a trap, in order to have a basis for accusing him. But Jesus bent down and started to write on the ground with his finger. [7]When they kept on questioning him, he straightened up and said to them, "If any one of you is without sin, let him*

"caretaking"

attempting to fix or rescue another person struggling with their own issues *be the first to throw a stone at her." ⁸Again he stooped down and wrote on the ground. ⁹At this, those who heard began to go away one at a time, the older ones first, until only Jesus was left, with the woman still standing there. ¹⁰Jesus straightened up and asked her, "Woman, where are they? Has no one condemned you?" ¹¹"No one, sir," she said. "Then neither do I condemn you," Jesus declared. "Go now and leave your life of sin." (John 8:4-11)*

In this story we have a woman who was filling herself up with sexual activity. She is being attacked by the leaders of the community who want to display their righteousness by stoning her in anger. (It is difficult for us to read this story without wondering how she came to be standing in the street without the partner she was caught in the act of sinning with but this may be a matter for another book.)

This passage is one of the best healing and recovery stories that we can use to gain new confidence about the power of God's love in relationship to His forgiveness of sin. The woman at the center of the struggle, her mistakes, the condemnation, and the humiliating attack brought to her by "religious" people all have a meaning that we need to examine in order to gain a better understanding of God.

She is literally dragged to Christ. She would not have come any other way. It is in her sexual mistake, her shame, and her guilt when under attack that she is forgiven by Christ. She is not forgiven because of anything she has done; rather, she is forgiven because Christ knows her heart. She has been freed from the death sentence. She is stolen away from death in the same way that every person in the angry mob may have been that day.

In that moment, they all learned something remarkable about God and about themselves. Many speculate about the role that the drawing in the sand plays in this story, but we have long been convinced that Christ was likely drawing symbols in Hebrew that inventoried the sins of each person who stood there, stone in hand, ready to execute this young woman.

In this story, Jesus revealed that the true path to forgiveness lies in recognizing and admitting your own sins. The mob could recognize the woman's sins, but not their own. After the intervention of Christ, they see one another's inventory written in the dirt and they are suddenly no longer the righteous and a sinner separated by the law, but children of God united in the forgiveness of their sin. It is interesting to note that those who had lived the longest lives left the stoning first.

4. Is your sin more like the woman in this story, or like the Pharisees? Or both? If so, how?

_____

_____

5. Have you ever compared your sin with those of others as either greater than or less than theirs? If so, can you give an example?

"making amends"

deciding upon a plan that will allow you to set a past injury or injustice at peace with another individual. it is not simply making an apology

If you do not see your own sin, you can go around bitterly condemning everyone and everything that has ever injured you. Your bitterness and anger will grow if you cannot relate to your own shortcomings. You will be unable to understand the fear, distress, and the weaknesses of others. If you do not see your own sin, you will not be able to forgive others in their weakness. Instead, we often rush to judge and sentence them despite our own inability to pay the price for what we have done. Jesus asks us to do our own inventory, accept His forgiveness, and trust in Him with the mistakes of our lives so that our healing can start. Then we can begin anew, no longer controlled by sin, shame, and guilt.

More questions for reflection

6) Can you think of a time in your life when you have treated someone harshly because of their sin? Can you think of a time in your life when someone has condemned you?

7. Is there someone in your life that you need to forgive today?

8. Have you forgiven yourself for your own mistakes of the past?

9. Is there someone in your life with whom you can share God's message of forgiveness? What has stopped you from reaching out to them in the past?

A final thought

Some years ago, a group of believers got together in an intercity neighborhood to start a church in a downtown bar. The bar owner willingly agreed since he didn't do much Sunday morning business anyway. The church promised that they would do the service in such a way that it would not interfere with his traffic. A few weeks later, people began to notice an elderly man who would come to the bar every Sunday morning. He never participated, but just sat with his back to the service. Before the service was over, he would be totally intoxicated. The church goers began to wonder what was wrong with him. Here we are, they thought, just a few feet away from him with a life-changing message that would rescue him from his self-destruction, but he won't participate!

In a less dramatic way, these kinds of situations happen in churches every Sunday. People get written off as lost or losers. Resentments may even begin to develop as compassion is replaced with frustration and anger toward people lost in sin.

There was one young man in this bar congregation who prayed for some word from God regarding the elderly man at the bar. The next Sunday, he sensed that God was asking him to share a very specific message with the older man. The young man was nervous because he did not understand the message, but he went ahead anyway. Putting his hand on the man's shoulder, he spoke these words into his drunken eyes…

"God killed His own Son too. He sees your pain and loves you!"

The man broke down into uncontrollable sobbing as a group of believers came around him. He told them that some years before he was cleaning his gun when a bright-eyed little boy came into the room and laughed "Shoot me Daddy!" Thinking that the gun was empty, he pretended to shoot him. Tragically, he killed his own son at point blank range. Since then, he had decided to kill himself a little bit at a time with alcohol.

The next week he came back to the little bar church sober and shaking, but visibly changed. It took someone with a heart for the broken to reveal God's message of forgiveness. It was a message that would not have been communicated by someone who had only sat in judgment of a man who simply needed to hear that God had forgiven him!

> *[12] How far has the LORD taken our sins from us? Farther than the distance from east to west! (Psalm 103:12)*

We can increase our ability to reach the lost if we accept God's forgiveness. Once we do, it allows us to heal and to share the message with those who are still trapped in religious legalism. Christ has already done the work; the free gift is ours.

"inventory"

a self-accounting of our own sin in terms of our relationship with God, not something we do on behalf of others

Devotional Verse: Forgiven and Loved

Read Romans 8: 31-39

Journaling Space:

transform

we learn to trust God and humbly ask Him to remove any self-imposed barriers that separate us from Him...

Read: Acts 9: 1-22 (Regaining our strength)

trans·form: verb
(Dictionary): To change appearance or form; to cause to change
(Faith): to become a new creation so we can live in the promise of His power

Many of us have come to this chapter sick and tired of the things in our lives that keep us from being better spouses, fathers, mothers, relatives, friends, or employees. Most of us would like to put all the pain and frustration behind us. If that's the case, the question is how does one do all that?

To begin the process, we need to recognize that the frustration that we have in our lives is most often associated with our own failures. Only when we can see our own anger, lust, fear overeating, drinking, procrastination, resentment, or gossip for what it really is... an issue of our own character, can we begin the transformation process. Many of us have gone through years of being ashamed, rejected, or troubled because of such issues. This is often because we didn't see our shortcomings as things that could be changed.

We may have spent decades nagging, pushing, isolating, lying, or raging on those people closest to us and not seeing the damage we were causing them (and ourselves) in the process. We may have been so hung up on our own symptoms that we overlook the likely cause, a series of issues deep within our own personality.

If we don't deal with these things, they will likely lead us right back to the kind of lives we don't want. For example, if we want to change a life that has been defined by overeating, but never deal with the things that make us want to eat too much, then we are missing out on real and meaningful life change. Transformation is not a diet for those that struggle with overeating. It is a process through which we can identify some of the issues that lead us to seek comfort from food in the first place.

People in drug recovery programs often talk about something that's important to understand if they want to grow in their faith. You'll hear them say that when they had their drugs taken away, all they had left was their unmanageable life. The absence of symptoms does not indicate health. We can be filled with cancer and feel just fine. Instead, we must look at

"serenity prayer"
a Christian prayer used in recovery circles that focuses on the need for us to accept things in our lives that we cannot control or change, while seeking courage to change those things within our control

those things that run our life when we are on autopilot. We can do this by asking ourselves a question. *How many decisions do I make unconsciously or simply out of habit?* Do I choose to react to someone in anger or is it an unconscious knee-jerk reaction? Am I habitually manipulated or injured by others? Am I selfish, afraid, jealous, isolated, depressed, stressed, manipulative, overbearing, insensitive, lonely, or impatient without even thinking about it? If so, we have things in our lives (even very subtle ones) that stand between us and who God wants us to be. We can correct them with His help.

The Bible repeatedly points to the promise of transformation. The International Standard Bible Encyclopedia[2] gives us a clear biblical sense of the meaning of the word as we see it used in most of the New Testament. It shows "transform" as translated from the Greek word for metamorphoomai (no need to try to pronounce it), from which we get the English word "metamorphosis" meaning a change in nature or appearance.

The definition goes on to say that this type of change is so complete that it surpasses the power of the word to describe it. We see this in nature when a caterpillar turns into a butterfly. The transformation is so miraculous that once complete, it is impossible to associate the two creatures in any way. There is no real scientific explanation for how a living creature can undergo such a complete change. But all things are possible with God.

In Luke, the disciples see Christ transformed before their very eyes from the man and teacher into what He really and truly is, the perfect and sinless Son of the Living God.

> *[28]About eight days after Jesus said this, he took Peter, John, and James with him and went up onto a mountain to pray. [29]As he was praying, the appearance of his face changed, and his clothes became as bright as a flash of lightning. [30]Two men, Moses and Elijah, [31]appeared in glorious splendor, talking with Jesus. They spoke about his departure, which he was about to bring to fulfillment at Jerusalem. [32]Peter and his companions were very sleepy, but when they became fully awake, they saw his glory and the two men standing with him. (Luke 9:28-32)*

Here, Jesus isn't just the man that they have walked with for three years with a bright light shining on Him. Suddenly, the disciples saw Christ in a completely new and miraculous way. He had been, and still is, totally transformed. The spiritual had replaced the physical and those walking with Christ saw His power and glory in a new way.

In the same way, we can read Biblical accounts of Jesus transforming the lame into those who can walk; the blind into those who can see; lepers into the healthy and the dead into the living. Christ constantly points us to the power of God to not just change something but to completely transform it. Such transformation is complete in the same way blindness has nothing in common with sight, disease with health or death with life. We see the same transformation in recovery and in churches that embrace the power of brokenness. When

---

[2] Copyright 1979 Wm. B. Eerdmans Publishing. Edited by Geoffrey W Bromiley

we hear testimonies of those whose lives have been transformed and then see it in their actions, we get undeniable confirmation of their transformations.

Transforming our own lives

Anyone on any meaningful journey of faith soon learns that we face a spiritual battle rather than a physical one. If we try to change our lives or to fight a spiritual war under our own strength, we will quickly find ourselves losing ground and creating an even larger mess in our lives. We can't win this battle based on the principles of self-help. But, when we fight this battle by enlisting His strength to aid us, we will become unstoppable. We become transformed not by our efforts alone, but by faith in the power of God.

> *38Then some of the Pharisees and teachers of the law said to him, "Teacher, we want to see a miraculous sign from you." 39He answered, "A wicked and adulterous generation asks for a miraculous sign! But none will be given it except the sign of the prophet Jonah. 40For as Jonah was three days and three nights in the belly of a huge fish, so the Son of Man will be three days and three nights in the heart of the earth.*
>
> *41The men of Nineveh will stand up at the judgment with this generation and condemn it; for they repented at the preaching of Jonah, and now one greater than Jonah is here. 42The Queen of the South will rise at the judgment with this generation and condemn it; for she came from the ends of the earth to listen to Solomon's wisdom, and now one greater than Solomon is here.*
>
> *43When an evil spirit comes out of a man; it goes through arid places seeking rest and does not find it. 44Then it says, 'I will return to the house I left.' When it arrives, it finds the house unoccupied, swept clean and put in order. 45Then it goes and takes with it seven other spirits more wicked than itself, and they go in and live there. And the final condition of that man is worse than the first. That is how it will be with this wicked generation." (Matthew 12:38-45)*

"baggage" figurative term for things that we carry with us from our own past or the past of others that slow or stop us in our recovery

The religious people of Christ's day rejected His message but asked Him to perform miracles to prove Himself to them. Christ instead gives them a history lesson and tells them that the only sign that He will give them is that of Jonah (which foreshadows the three days that He will spend in darkness between His death and resurrection). On the surface, they seem to be looking for Christ to change something before their eyes so they can believe in Him. But, they are not coming with a personal desire to glorify God, to seek life change or to see the truth, *but to discredit Him*. They want to see change without putting any personal effort, faith or hope into the process themselves.

There is something special about this passage that will help us apply it to our journey of faith. Christ is being asked to prove Himself. It would be like walking up to a man who is wearing a navy uniform while weighing anchor on a destroyer and asking him to prove that he was a sailor. These Pharisees and teachers of the law were surrounded by eye witnesses every day and were fully aware of the accounts of miracles Jesus had performed. He had healed lepers, cured the blind, made the lame walk, raised people from the dead, turned water into wine and had great crowds following Him wherever He went. In reality, they were not asking Christ for a sign so that they could believe. They were looking for reasons to support the fact that they already had rejected Him. They were not looking to be transformed into believers, they wanted to transform the God of the universe into a magician at best and at worst into a man that they could label a liar.

The Pharisees and teachers of the law in the story are in many ways representative of what's wrong in most western religions. They approached Christ as people who believed that they were without sin and that they had the power to be in a relationship with God based on their works and knowledge of the law. Given such an attitude, they likely would have rejected Jesus no matter how many miracles He performed.

In responding to them, Jesus paints a picture of how hopeless it can be to engage in a spiritual battle without God's help. Apart from God, our efforts to permanently change under our own power will always fail. But, when we take all the junk in our lives, no matter how big or small it is, and put it in God's hands, humbly asking Him to take it away, He will transform us.

Biblical reference

If anyone ever understood this, it was the Apostle Paul. In an attempt to admit the reality of the sin in his life and how much he needed to rely on Christ he wrote:

[18]I know that nothing good lives in me, that is, in my sinful nature for I have the desire to do what is good, but I cannot carry it out. [19]For what I do is not the good I want to do; no, the evil I do not want to do—this I keep on doing. [20]Now if I do what I do not want to do, it is no longer I who do it, but it is sin living in me that does it. [21]So I find this law at work: when I want to do good, evil is right there with me. [22]For in my inner being I delight in God's law; [23]but I see another law at work in the members of my body, waging war against the law of my mind and making me a prisoner of the law of sin at work within my members. [24]What a wretched man I am! Who will rescue me from this body of death? [25]Thanks be to God—through Jesus Christ our Lord! So then, I myself in my mind am a slave to God's law, but in the sinful nature a slave to the law of sin. (Romans 7:15-25)

Paul understands that if he does not recognize the sin in his life, he will return to the place where he started as a man who was as much addicted to religion as someone might be addicted to drugs. This doesn't mean being subjected to the guilt and shame of sin. It means recognizing that it is part of your life and requires a Savior in order to be forgiven. When we don't understand this, we become like the people in churches who reject hurting people and fail to reach out to them. Sadly, that failure is the biggest reason why so many people hate churches and the people in them.

1. How does Paul's testimony of struggle relate to your current situation?

_____

_____

_____

_____

_____

"H.A.L.T." an acronym for the discipline not to make life changing decisions when we are hungry, angry, lonely, or tired

Paul (then Saul) himself certainly had one of the most significant transformations in the entire Bible. While on the road to Damascus, (on his way to persecute Christians), a light from heaven flashed around him. As he fell to the ground, he heard a voice say to him, "Saul, Saul, why do you persecute me?" When he got up from the ground, he couldn't see anything for three days. Then the Lord sent a disciple, Ananias, to help him. Ananias placed his hands on Saul and confirmed that it was Christ who had appeared to him on the road. He also told him that he had been sent so that Paul would be filled with the Holy Spirit. Immediately, Paul could see again. He got up and was baptized before eating. He then spent several days with the disciples in Damascus, preaching in the synagogues that Jesus is the Son of God. Our own transformations may or may not be as dramatic but can be equally as important.

Hoping for better things

Christ assures us that if we place our trust in Him, we can have a life that is free from slavery to the things that we hate to do. Does this mean that nothing bad will ever happen to us again and that we will be free from further temptation and sin? No. But we must come to believe two things, first that all sin past and future is forgiven in Christ and second, that anything bad that does happen to us can be turned into a greater good by God.

God will not take anything away from His children unless He intends to give them something better. Does it mean that we will never be sick again or that we will be instantly healed if we trust in God? No, but it does mean that in our sickness or health, we can be a witness to the kingdom of God. That "better thing" may not be apparent during our lives on this earth, but still waiting for us in heaven just the same. When we come to God in His will and in unity as believers, He has a miraculous promise waiting for us.

> *[19] "Again, I tell you that if two of you on earth agree about anything you ask for, it will be done for you by my Father in heaven. [20] For where two or three come together in my name, there am I with them."*
> (Matthew 18:19-20)

If we come together to seek an understanding of God's will, agreeing as a community to come to Him to ask for His help on His terms, Christ is telling us that it will be done. So, if two or three of us should get together based on this passage and agree that we deserve to win the lottery, will we? This is obviously not what Jesus is telling us here. He is saying that if it is within His will, it glories Him and it is in the context of healing the church body, then it will be given.

After all, is it in God's will that we live in fear? No. Is it in God's will that we suffer with unhealthy lifestyles; to be beaten by an abusive spouse or to kill ourselves slowly with drugs, anger, work, food, or alcohol? No. Is it God's will that we spend hours looking at pornography while our marriages and children suffer? Clearly it is not!

2. If you are in a small group, are you actively taking part or are you just showing up?

_____

_____

_____

_____

_____

We as Christians don't always take God up on this promise to transform us. But, why not? It would seem that our desire to seek His will is often sabotaged by our own wishes to continue doing whatever we want when we want. To truly transform ourselves, we must decide to identify the things in our lives that God is revealing to us that require change and become willing to change them.

In the opening chapter on denial, we were asked to admit that we have unmanageable lives. In this chapter, we want to identify *exactly why* our lives continue to be unmanageable. Perhaps it is:

Because we lie or live in deceit?
Because we are controlling other people or are controlled by someone else? ----
Because we live in fear?

Because we are bitter?
Because we overeat?
Because we act out sexually?
Because we drink too much?
Because we are angry?
Because we use drugs?
Because money is our god?
Because we are self-centered?
Because we are codependent (a people pleaser)?
Because we habitually place people, places, and things before God?
Because we _____?

To really transform ourselves, we need to act in the confidence that we have in Christ to deal with the destructive habits that have taken over our lives. Habits are recurrent, often unconscious patterns of behavior brought about through frequent repetition. Left unmanaged, habits become part of our character. (We can also describe an addiction to drugs, alcohol, internet pornography, overeating and other unhealthy things as "habits".) We can have full confidence in our forgiveness through God's mercy and grace. At the same time, we also need to understand that our shortcomings, if not removed and replaced with acceptable habits, will cause us to return to the behaviors we hate. We must also understand that these habits are not really the problem, but only leftover symptoms of a disease that God has already cured when we accept Christ.

"fixing"

interfering with another person's recovery in an effort to hasten or control their progress

If we truly want release from the past and peace for today, we need to face our problems head on. Successful transformation requires an honest evaluation of the things that we don't like about ourselves. If we want to be free of our resentment, our anger, our bitterness, our lies, our viewing pornography, our cheating, our overeating, our drinking or whatever else has become unmanageable in our lives, we need to make a specific list of exactly what we want to overcome. This is something that really can't be done alone. It usually requires the help of an accountability partner (a person of faith who understands these principles) to help us inventory our negative habits. When we are able to clearly identify what specific things are adversely affecting our lives, we can become willing to humbly ask God to remove our shortcomings.

> *⁵If any of you lacks wisdom, he should ask God, who gives generously to all without finding fault, and it will be given to him. ⁶But when he asks, he must believe and not doubt, because he who doubts is like a wave of the sea, blown and tossed by the wind. (James 1: 5-6)*

Another former small group member once shared this about his own past:

> "In my life this required an honest assessment of the things I was doing that continually pulled me into the past. It was a fight dominated by the pain of the past to a new life lived in the promise of the day. It was at this point in my healing that I realized that I had two primary issues that needed to be addressed. I was

constantly angry and defensive. My defensiveness led to rage. My rage confirmed to the outside world that I was unstable. The instability came back to me as a confirmation of my unworthiness and mistrust of people. It led to an ongoing feeling of anger and desire to be isolated. (Isolation for people in recovery eventually leads them to act out again.)

The second big issue I needed to face was a habit of constantly lying. I had developed this as a safety mechanism. It was a destructive habit that had taken on a life of its own. I would lie about everything, important or not. The lies were always aimed at preserving an image that was not in keeping with the new life I was trying to live. I wanted to be interesting and popular. I never wanted to be caught doing anything that could be construed as wrong. I never wanted to face my part in things. If I was late for an appointment because I overslept, there had to have been a car accident, a power failure, or a major problem with the alarm clock. I lied about my past, my preferences, and my boring trips to the grocery store. Every time I lied about something the effect was clear, it would come back to me again and again, causing me to feel that I was totally unworthy of forgiveness."

We need to think about our destructive habits like diseases such as cancer or leprosy. As such, each must be taken seriously! Both are progressive and destructive in nature. Like diseases left untreated, our destructive habits will disfigure us, separate us from relationships or even eventually kill us. Like sickness, our destructive habits need to be diagnosed and healed. When we see it this way, it becomes clear that we need to become willing to ask the "Great Physician" (God) for the restoration we need.

> *[11] When the Pharisees saw this, they asked his disciples, "Why does your teacher eat with tax collectors and 'sinners'?" [12] On hearing this, Jesus said, "It is not the healthy who need a doctor, but the sick. [13] But go and learn what this means: 'I desire mercy, not sacrifice.' For I have not come to call the righteous, but sinners". (Matthew 9:11-13)*

As God works in your life, celebrate, and share praises with the people you love and those in your community of faith to get some encouragement about what you have received. If you have not done this yet, work towards it diligently. It is one of the true milestones in creating the life that God wants for you. We are not just experiencing a simple life change; we are being transformed by a power greater than ourselves!

3. What destructive habits are you struggling with today? List them.

_____

_____

4. Do you have habits in your life right now that you would like to change? If so, where do you think they originated? What is your earliest recollection of them?

5. Do you believe that you need God's help to become willing?

6. What is stopping you from asking God to remove your shortcomings?

7. Write a prayer that asks God to help you identify exactly what you need to change.

_____

_____

_____

_____

_____

miracle

we humbly asked Him to remove all our shortcomings...

Read: Matthew 9:1-8 (Our forgiveness is part of His power to do miracles)

miracle: noun
(Dictionary): any amazing or wonderful occurrence
(Faith): a divine interruption of God's established laws of nature to reach or create change in the lives of His people

As we continue our journey through the language of healing, we will now focus our attention on a word that is often misunderstood in both Christian and secular circles. That word is "miracle". Since our journey of faith can be described as a progression of miracles, and our faith placed in those miracles, it is important that we gain a biblical understanding what the word really means.

For many of us in recovery, it was a miracle that we sought any help at all! If we talked to the people closest to us they probably would have been surprised that we had finally sought help. It's rare to meet anyone with a living testimony of life change who doesn't have a story that points to some kind of divine intervention.

Seeing God

The miracles continue when we take the time to discover who God is and make the decision to turn our will and our lives over to His care. As believers, taking self-centered lives and turning them into God-centered ones overflowing with love are miracles of the purest form indeed!

One of the goals we have in our journey towards healing is to seek (and find) permanent life change. In order for us to approach God and ask Him to remove our shortcomings we need a basic understanding of who He is and how much He loves us. Most of us develop our ideas about who God is from our image of our earthly father. For many of us, this is a huge part of the battle. Somewhere along the way someone has injured us. For some of us, our relationship with our own earthly father was the source of that damage. He may have abused us, abandoned us, or turned to drugs and alcohol. Some of us grew up with no model for a loving advocate who loves us and cares about the details of our lives. It can be very hard to search for miraculous intervention when we don't trust the source.

Some of us were damaged under the pretense of religion. Some of us were heaped with shame and guilt and told that we were sentenced to eternal damnation because of our past transgressions. Others of us just wonder how a loving God could allow all sorts of bad

---

"what we say here stays here"

regarding confidentiality, the assurance that we have privacy and safety in our sharing time so that we no longer need to live with secrets

things to happen to us or others.

God has a plan for our lives. He loves all of His children so much that He will not remove our eternal promise. That promise is found in our freedom to choose between darkness and light. He promises that if we trust in Him, He will make even the things intended to do us harm to be used for the greater good. When you look around the room in a true gathering of believers you might see people who have lied, manipulated, stolen and cheated; people who have killed others and people who have themselves been injured, abandoned, abused, or beaten. In each life, God is working a miracle that is turning their pain into peace. If we start looking at our difficulties through the eyes of God, we will see that these things are really opportunities to create a better life for us here on earth and eternal joy for us in heaven. However, this will only happen if we trust in the promise. If we do not trust, the miracles are meaningless. Getting to the miracle means living through the pain and rejoicing in the assurance of God's answer.

In Christ, there is no death without resurrection. Similarly, there can be no miracle without a problem. Speaker and writer John Maxwell tells people who go to God in pain that they will find good news, that God is about to do something miraculous. To experience this fully, we must come as those ready to suffer and count it as joy. It is when we are in such a mindset that God can do more than we can ask or imagine.

Christ tells us that if our minds and hearts are closed to God, no number of miracles, arguments or revelations will ever reach us. But, only when we are broken and searching for release from our guilt, shame and hurt can we clearly see the message of His love. Only then, can we embrace it like we have never held onto anything before. It is with the same intensity that we hung onto the pain of our past that we can cling to the promises and forgiveness of Christ. When we accept Him, nothing can separate us from the promise of forgiveness or from the miracles that He has waiting for those with an open heart.

Separating ourselves from the past

It is only when we are in a relationship with God and understand His plan for us if we will just stop fighting with Him, that He will give us the courage to face the issues of our past. To help separate ourselves from the past it is critical for us not just to look at our faults, but to actually write them down. It is when we see them in black and white that we can best summon the courage to share this "inventory" with God and another person. If you find this extremely difficult to accomplish, we can say with confidence that this is exactly what you need to do to heal and to grow in your relationship with Christ!

Writing it down has incredible power. When we write down our inventory, when we journal or when we take the time to write our thoughts and feelings to others, we release a new power in our lives that is so awesome that it is difficult to describe. It will be a miracle!

When we look at this from a biblical perspective, we see God using the inspired words of people to reach billions throughout the ages. We have thousands of pages of testimonies, letters, stories, and recollections that represent the lives and ministries of those who have gone before us. (When Nehemiah rebuilt the walls of Jerusalem, he left a lasting record of his achievement in the form of a diary.) In fact, the Bible is for the most part a collection of revelations, stories, diaries, and letters. It is the work of people recording their struggles, pains, and praises in the power of divine revelation.

Christ himself never wrote anything. He left the task of recording how He changed lives to those whose lives had been affected. It is when we write down our hopes, fears, dreams, prayers, and shortcomings that God can work in our lives in a miraculous way. No matter where you are in your journey of faith and healing, writing down your thoughts and feelings will bring you a new and profound growth, peace, and freedom. Doing so gives God a greater opportunity to heal us, and when we are ready, journaling our thoughts helps us better share them with others.

The miracle of healing

For people attempting to change their lives, healing and recovery may seem like the hardest thing they have ever done. But, in comparison to the demands of living a life ruled by shame, guilt or addictive behavior, it is light work. Choosing the path of faith is easy when we compare it to the bondage of food, anger, workaholism, alcohol, codependent acting out, addiction to pornography or to the emptiness of life without a living faith in God.

Often, as a person gets closer to healing, old habits sometimes seem to work against all they are trying to accomplish. They may still have a temper that is seemingly uncontrollable. They may still be fighting addiction to food, work, sex, alcohol, or drugs. They may not yet have the faith they want. They may still have doubts that prevent them from coming into a new season of faith. Some of them will have to let go of any predetermined outcomes and just trust in God to provide what they need. Some of them may have to struggle longer and harder than others to achieve healing and recovery, but that miracle will come.

There are no small miracles. Every miracle is significant because of how it can change someone's life. There are no small miracles in God's economy. Even your ability to put just some of your issues behind you opens the door for God to use you in a powerful way. For example, God removing a father's rage or desire to control may be exactly the witness that his teenage children need to accept Christ. The miracle of recovery will change your life, but it also can make a huge difference in the lives of others around you. One life changed can change tens of thousands of other lives.

Keep in mind that God's biggest miracles can happen only in the midst of crisis or pain. For the miracle of the parting of the Red Sea to have the importance that it had, the children of Israel needed to stand defenseless with their backs to the sea with no apparent hope of escape. Ironically, even with the dramatically parted waves, many of them would not have crossed to the other side if Pharaoh's chariots had not been chasing them. Deep in crisis,

"program"
the way in which we live our faith, work our recovery and lead our lives

they were not seeing God's plan to destroy what had oppressed them for so long.

Biblical reference

God wants us to identify our problems, so we can take hold of His power to heal us. There is an interesting and often overlooked miracle in the Old Testament that will help us clearly see how God wants to work in our lives:

> *[38] Elisha returned to Gilgal and there was a famine in that region. While the company of the prophets was meeting with him, he said to his servant, "Put on the large pot and cook some stew for these men." [39] One of them went out into the fields to gather herbs and found a wild vine. He gathered some of its gourds and filled the fold of his cloak. When he returned, he cut them up into the pot of stew, though no one knew what they were. [40] The stew was poured out for the men, but as they began to eat it, they cried out, "O man of God, there is death in the pot!" And they could not eat it. [41] Elisha said, "Get some flour." He put it into the pot and said, "Serve it to the people to eat." And there was nothing harmful in the pot. (2 Kings 4:38-41)*

This story teaches us a number of things that we need to think about as we ask God to take away things that threaten to kill us physically, spiritually, or emotionally. *In other words, we need to be able to see the poison in our lives.* We must understand that He is more than capable of removing such poison from us.

These prophets were starving and it would have been just as easy to ignore the unpleasant taste and fill their stomachs. Instead, they recognized what they were trying to fill themselves with was poison that would eventually kill them. They chose life over death. In our own lives we need to see what is poisoning us spiritually. Then we need to ask God to purify us by removing those shortcomings.

> *[9] If we confess our sins; he is faithful and just and will forgive us our sins and purify us from all unrighteousness. (I John 1:9)*

In this account, we have people who believe they have been poisoned by something they had just eaten. In this miracle, Elisha overcomes death with flour, by throwing good food (flour) into the bad food. They would have thought it quite foolish to waste precious flour in the middle of famine by tossing it into poison. However, when we look at any miracle, the tool used for transformation (flour in this case) may often be as important as the act itself.

Flour comes to us in an interesting way. A seed needs to be buried or "sacrificed" so that new life can emerge. It is much like death and resurrection. The sacrifice of the one produces a hundred times the seed. That seed is then crushed so that it can be used to sustain life. Bread was used in the ministry of Christ to demonstrate His power to forgive and heal us. In Old Testament times, flour was placed at the altar to atone for sin.

When we take communion, broken bread is used to symbolize how His body was crushed to produce an opportunity for eternal life. Christ was crushed so that everyone could be filled, so that death could be taken away from us regardless of our sin. The promise is for everyone. In God's economy, there is no death without a resurrection. There are no problems without solutions. There is no pain that cannot be used to strengthen ourselves and others. No matter where you are right now, if you trust in God you will be reborn today. Your broken past will be given glory in relationship with God. Your sins, shame and guilt are washed away. The poison will be removed if you trust in Him.

are we gathering trouble or is someone bringing it to us?

Where does the poison come from in this story? When a person is hungry, troubled, or injured, they are often tempted to wander off and find anything that looks good and toss it into the pot in order to spice up their life. Did the person picking the poison intend to injure everyone else? No, not intentionally, they were simply looking for a way to be filled in a time of spiritual famine.

It's good to consider this story when we look at pain caused by someone else's acting out and how it may have set the stage for bad choices we've made. People act out on us and hurt us for what it does for them, not the pain that it causes us. *"Hurt people hurt people"* as the saying goes. They too, need to heal, receiving their miracle and escaping from the death that they have chosen in their lives. We can better overcome our own shame, pain, and anger if we will compassionately pray for and forgive those who have injured us. When we can forgive them, it will be easier to accept forgiveness ourselves.

Healing does not always happen the way that we think it should, but it's always a miracle!

"transparency"
honest and open sharing about who we are, including our shortcomings

Questions for reflection

1. What are the things in my life that I want to be free of?

_____

_____

_____

_____

2. Do I trust God to heal me? If not, who can I talk to about my faith?

_____

_____

_____

_____

3. What miracles have I seen that can help me place my trust in God?

_____

_____

_____

_____

4. Is there someone of faith who I can ask to share their miracle with me?

_____

_____

_____

relationship

we made a list of all persons we had harmed or who had injured us and became willing to make amends to them all...

Read: Colossians 3: 9-13 (Bearing with each other)

re·la·tion·ship: noun
(Dictionary): being related, connected, or associated in some way
(Faith): an association with Christ-centered people or groups that allows us to become healthy by focusing on God's plan for our lives

To advance this far in our journey, we've needed to exercise our faith repeatedly and use it to admit our brokenness. We used it to come to find a living relationship with God and to turn our will and our lives over to Him. We used our faith to overcome our fear of separating ourselves from the past. We used it to fearlessly take our own inventory and share it with God and another person. Then we used our faith to humbly look at our own destructive habits and ask God to remove them from us.

Now, we will need to depend on our faith in a new way as we come to one of the most difficult areas we may ever face in our healing, that of interpersonal relationships. To move forward in faith, one eventually has to face relationship issues with family, friends, coworkers, and others. If we are going to be truly liberated from the past and be able to honestly share our experience, strength, and hope with others, we will have to first deal with the pain of our past relationships. There is no better test of our faith in Jesus Christ than how we handle ourselves when we have wronged someone or someone else has hurt us.

We can begin to improve our current and past relationships in two ways:

- By becoming willing to make amends
- By becoming willing to offer forgiveness

When we become willing, we can gain freedom from the relational pain in our lives. The key word here is *willing*, because only when we become willing can we really begin to put the hurt, shame, and guilt behind us forever. In the chapter on Community, we'll further explore the concept of actually making our amends.

No matter where we are in our journey, we can make a conscious choice to avoid unhealthy relationships and replace them with ones that build us up. This is extremely important for all believers and lifesaving for people who want to put addictions behind them. We can *choose* to stop living in the past. We can *decide* to stop letting poor decisions or abusive people

"testimony"
a speaking opportunity for an individual to share their experience, strength and hope and the resulting life change with others

control our actions and relationships. We can *make a choice* to stop being stuck in the pain of bad relationships and past mistakes. But, if not, we will by default choose to remain stuck in the trauma and bitterness of bad relationships and spend less time developing a relationship with God.

It's not easy dealing with issues of relationship, but answers can be found if we look to Christ for direction. He sums up the key to all successful relationships in 11 words...

> [31]*Do to others as you would have them do to you". (Luke 6:31)*

During Jesus' time on this earth, the opposite, "Do not do to others as you would not want done to you" was a common expression. He took this idea of passively not harming another individual and turned it into a statement of action and care. Understanding this can be an important turning point for us. We can forgive and make amends or we can allow the past, with all its bitterness and anger, to rule our lives. If we choose the first, we heal; if we choose the second, we separate ourselves from accepting all of God's love and stand the risk of returning to the behaviors that we very much want to escape.

Biblical reference

In the 15th chapter of Luke, Jesus teaches us about restoring damaged relationships. He shows us how people are injured and injure others:

> [11]*Jesus continued: "There was a man who had two sons.* [12]*The younger one said to his father, 'Father, give me my share of the estate.' So, he divided his property between them.* [13]*Not long after that, the younger son got together all he had, set off for a distant country and there squandered his wealth in wild living.* [14]*After he had spent everything, there was a severe famine in that whole country, and he began to be in need.* [15]*So he went and hired himself out to a citizen of that country, who sent him to his fields to feed pigs.* [16]*He longed to fill his stomach with the pods that the pigs were eating, but no one gave him anything.*
>
> [17]*When he came to his senses, he said, 'How many of my father's hired men have food to spare, and here I am starving to death!* [18]*I will set out and go back to my father and say to him: Father, I have sinned against heaven and against you.* [19]*I am no longer worthy to be called your son; make me like one of your hired men.'* [20]*So he got up and went to his father. "But while he was still a long way off, his father saw him and was filled with compassion for him; he ran to his son, threw his arms around him, and kissed him.*
>
> [21]*The son said to him, 'Father, I have sinned against heaven and against*

you. I am no longer worthy to be called your son." ²²But the father said to his servants, 'Quick! Bring the best robe and put it on him. Put a ring on his finger and sandals on his feet. ²³Bring the fattened calf and kill it. Let's have a feast and celebrate. ²⁴For this son of mine was dead and is alive again; he was lost and is found.' So, they began to celebrate.

²⁵Meanwhile, the older son was in the field. When he came near the house, he heard music and dancing. ²⁶So he called one of the servants and asked him what was going on. ²⁷'Your brother has come,' he replied, 'and your father has killed the fattened calf because he has him back safe and sound.' ²⁸The older brother became angry and refused to go in. So, his father went out and pleaded with him. ²⁹But he answered his father, 'Look! All these years I've been slaving for you and never disobeyed your orders. Yet you never gave me even a young goat so I could celebrate with my friends. ³⁰But when this son of yours who has squandered your property with prostitutes comes home, you kill the fattened calf for him!' ³¹'My son,' the father said, 'you are always with me, and everything I have is yours. ³²But we had to celebrate and be glad, because this brother of yours was dead and is alive again; he was lost and is found.'"
(Luke 15:11-32)

"relapse"
a return to the behavior(s) that you attempted to overcome

Among other things, this story is about being willing to make amends. With the understanding that all of us have been injured or have injured someone else, let's take a closer look at each character in the story to see just how much injury there is to go around.

The father is injured by both of his sons. The youngest injures him by his absence, for squandering his inheritance and rejecting the father's values; the older for his bitterness toward him and his younger son.

The oldest son believes that he has been injured by both the father and the youngest son. He thinks that his father has unfairly favored his younger brother by giving him something that he didn't deserve. He is also injured by his brother because he took advantage of his father. His injury is further deepened when the younger brother comes back home displacing what he thinks is his.

The younger son is injured by his employer who leaves him to starve in squalor. He is also injured by his older brother who refuses to acknowledge him when he returns and later tries to pull his father away from him.

The employer was injured by the younger son, who we can assume abandons his work without notice and leaves no one to feed his pigs when he departs!

Here, Jesus is teaching us why we need to forgive and ask for forgiveness as well. Every one of us has damaged someone, somewhere, because of our actions… regardless of how "right" it may have seemed at the time. Christ is telling us that we are all guilty of destroying and damaging relationships and that it is our responsibility to try to repair them. It is also our responsibility to forgive others just as the father figure in the story forgives his son. If we have been injured we must be willing to forgive, and if we have injured someone, we must be willing to ask for their forgiveness.

Three kinds of people

It is important not to run out and apologize to people or forgive them without first seeking God's heart. This helps us be clear about our motives. Before we do anything, we need to become truly willing to do so. We also need to fully understand the nature of the relationships that we attempt to mend. Not all people have the same motives, nor should they be dealt with in the same way. As we become more willing to make amends, it is important that we pray and seek God's direction before we approach each person.

To begin the process, the relationships in question must be divided into one of three categories. Only then can they be acted upon within a scriptural framework. With these three categories as a guide, we can begin to look at our part in the relational history of our lives and face it for what it really is.

1. People who are actively damaging us or our children *(those who are wicked)*
FOR TRUE LIFE CHANGE, SEPARATE YOURSELF FROM THE WICKED
(But extend an opportunity for restoration)

2. People who are lazy, undependable, gossips or draining *(those who are fools)*
MINISTER TO, BUT DO NOT DEPEND ON FOOLS
(But witness to them and extend encouragement)

3. People seeking the truth *(those who are righteous)*
SURROUND YOURSELF WITH THE RIGHTEOUS
(But be accountable, measuring your associations on God's word and direction)

The oldest son acts out in his wickedness in attacking his brother. The younger brother is foolish as he takes what is not really his and squanders it; he chooses poorly and stays on that path until he is starving to death in a pig pen. His change only comes in his brokenness, not from anything else. The father represents the righteous in this story. He runs out to embrace not only his foolish son, but he also meets his wicked son in the field and reminds him of his position in the family. Here, Jesus is teaching us that it is our brokenness that returns us to favor with God and that our self-centeredness can only leave us even more isolated and bitter.

Slaves to our problems

The younger son's plight is a model recovery story. He separates himself from the care and love of a father who truly desires to have a relationship with him. He wastes his talents and the treasures for temporary gratification. When he realizes what he has done wrong, he becomes a slave to his problem. Many of us do this in our own lives when we are injured by someone else, (domestic abuse, sexually assaulted, or verbally abused, etc.) and allow it to become the entire basis of our identity. Many of us have done this very thing to ourselves and others in our selfishness.

In the story we see the young man returning home not as a free man who will be forgiven for what he has done, but as a slave to the poor choices of the past. He has convinced himself that he will need to work the rest of his life to please his father. This is exactly how satan wants us to see God in our time of need as someone who can never be pleased, who is harshly judgmental and who wants to keep us in the chains of defeat. It is also how satan wants us to view each other, as people steeped in resentments who are not available for restoration.

However, Jesus gives us a much different picture of how God (His Father) actually is. The father, (representing God in this story) who knew better than his son, humbles himself to run to his son. He ignores the filthy rags and the smell and rushes to embrace the boy. He restores him to his position as a son based on his immense love and compassion for the boy. He liberates his son from the self-imposed slavery of his actions by accepting his apology. God wants to do this for all of us, no matter how far we think we have strayed from Him. It is God's love combined with the sacrifice of Christ that is enough to assure us we too can be restored.

We are all the Older and the Younger Brother
If we look closely, we can see ourselves in the two brothers. Like the younger brother, we often expect to receive only good things, even if it is not right for us. If we do get what we want and then misuse those things, we are likely to let them separate us from God who is our real source of happiness and joy. We will linger in the "pig pens" of life for weeks, months or even years before we will be broken enough to come home. (Many of us will reach out to others and try to drag them into our pig pen so we are not alone there.) Ultimately, we will need to stand up in our brokenness and reach out to God because we can always count on Him to forgive us.

Like the older brother, we question God when we don't get what we think we deserve while someone else is getting what looks like a free pass. We shake our fist at God or separate ourselves from Him like pouting children. We seek to be forgiven for all of our own sin but draw the line for others. They don't deserve a good life, fellowship, family, or forgiveness because they killed someone, drank, abused, left, raged, cheated, or violated us somehow. But despite all that, we must still forgive them.

> *⁴If he sins against you seven times in a day, and seven times comes back to you and says, 'I repent,' forgive him." (Luke 17:4)*

These are easy words to say, but hard to do. Removed from Christ's power, they are impossible. *This is because the key to forgiving is about first embracing our own*

"authentic community"
a church body in which transparency, brokenness before the Lord and healing are core values

forgiveness and then from that place of grace extending it to others. (See Matthew 18: 23-35.) People will almost never ask you to forgive them, so we must be willing to take the first step. But we can do this only when we are at peace based on the forgiveness that we ourselves have received from God. No matter who we are, what we have done or what has been done to us, we must rely on Christ for an eternal relationship with a loving God. God sees our worth based on how He sees us in Christ and not on anything that we have done. He wants to wrap His arms around us and love us with a love that is so strong, so eternal and so unconditional that, in our humanness, we can never fully understand it.

Taking action

Make a list of the people who have harmed you or those you have harmed and place those relationships in God's hands. When we submit our relationships to Him, we may still find ourselves in conflict, but this will only serve to strengthen our faith, not weaken it. Remember the price Christ paid to forgive us so we can separate ourselves from the pain, guilt, and shame of the past.

> *[10] The thief comes only to steal and kill and destroy; I have come that they may have life and have it to the full. (John 10:10)*

Living a life filled with peace and the good things that God wants us to have is a choice. When we are surrounded with pain, loss and doubt we need to understand that satan is using these things to destroy us. When we become willing to give these areas of our life to God, we can be secure in the knowledge that He is fully capable of making all things work together for good, no matter how bad things might seem today.

> *[27] And he who searches our hearts knows the mind of the Spirit, because the Spirit intercedes for the saints in accordance with God's will. [28] And we know that in all things God works for the good of those who love him, who have been called according to his purpose. (Romans 8:27-28)*

Faith grows through trial. As we overcome our issues, we grow deeper and stronger in our faith. Then, based on how we overcome the junk in our own lives, we can be used to inspire others to accept Christ. We are truly blessed in our afflictions; for they give us the power to grow in faith and to show us that we are truly experiencing life change in God's power and not in our own.

Questions for reflection

1. Do you believe that you can be forgiven without forgiving?

2. What part have you played in the relationships that you have damaged?

3. If you have been injured by others, what do you now believe about their intentions?

4. Do you harbor bitterness or resentment towards anyone today?

_____
_____
_____
_____

5. How does the world tend to judge people's value or worth?

_____
_____
_____
_____

6. How does God see your worth?

_____
_____
_____
_____

Devotional

How should we seek forgiveness? Read the parable of the pharisee and the tax collector in Luke 18: 9-14.

community

we made direct amends to such people whenever possible, except when to do so would injure them or others...

Read: 2Corinthians 5:17-20 (The old has gone and the new has come)

com mun ity: noun
(Dictionary): a group of people having common interests or a common location; collectivism
(Faith): sharing, support, forgiveness, and fellowship built on the foundation of Christ's grace; God's community or family

As we try to move from the influence of our hurts, hang-ups, and habits to a place of healing and strength, we can begin to close the door on things of the past. In fact, the very issues that have destroyed the peace of our present and our hope for the future can be used to help us heal along with others in a supportive Christ-centered community. Or we can let those things isolate us from the very people who can help us repair the damage.

Our modern culture usually defines a community by its geographical limits. In faith terms, community doesn't have anything to do with physical proximity. To fully understand what we are describing here, let's consider the biblical definition of what community is. The Hebrew translation paints a picture of help, support, and emotional involvement. Its origin is in another Hebrew word that gives us insight into what an authentic community looks like:

Ga'ah: **to rise up, grow up, be exalted in triumph**

The function of an authentic family or biblical community is one of sharing, support, participation and fellowship. The vast majority of the issues and baggage that most people bring into healing and recovery comes from some sort of dysfunctional community relationship. A prime example of this might be one's family of origin where there were unresolved issues of abandonment, alcoholism, or abuse. That shared experience and support for one another found in authentic Christian "families" forms the basis of true biblical community.

> *[10] If one falls down, his friend can help him up. But pity the man who falls and has no one to help him up! (Ecclesiastes 4:10)*

It then becomes obvious why the evil one would want to discourage us from becoming part of such a community and why he would attack us once we are in it. satan wants to use our past and present to stop us from growing in our faith in God by trying to get us to:

"journal"
a written record of your thoughts that helps you process your feelings

- Harshly judge the motives of other believers
- Doubt our support of one another.
- Falsely believe that we have been permanently separated from God.
- Do other "self-help" things in an attempt to gain the peace we desire.
- Harbor so much resentment and anxiety that no one can minister to us.
- Be in a place of distraction and distress that disconnects us emotionally.
- Let pettiness, gossip or misplaced advice from others discourage us.
- Isolate ourselves from believers who can contribute to our walk of faith.
- Allow malice or injury to separate us from a loving and supportive place.

God's perspective on community

Christ's Sermon on the Mount teaches us about protecting, nurturing, and preserving authentic community. We are taught that sin will divide and destroy a community of believers:

> *[21]"You have heard that it was said to the people long ago, 'Do not murder, and anyone who murders will be subject to judgment.' [22]But I tell you that anyone who is angry with his brother will be subject to judgment. Again, anyone who says to his brother, 'Raca' is answerable to the Sanhedrin. But anyone who says, 'You fool!' will be in danger of the fire of hell." (Matthew 5:21-22)*

What Jesus is saying here is to look to God and not to ourselves for provision, moral clarity, and forgiveness. He is also pointing out something that many of us know through painful experience, that the consequences of sin in our lives will separate us from God and prevent healing. If we lead lives of anger, pride, or resentment, we will be dominated by these things. The Pharisees, (the keepers and teachers of the law who Christ is referring to in this passage), are examples of people who want to cover themselves with all the trappings that look good but who really aren't.

God wants us to understand that He measures us not so much by what we are doing but by our heart. Authentic Christianity is not, be good and be accepted. It is "come to me with an open heart" and be guided, directed, and be forgiven regardless of your failures. The heart is what God uses to measure who we truly are. Can we have a good heart and do the wrong thing? Yes. Can we try to look like we are doing the right thing with a heart filled with spite for others around us? Yes!

Jesus helps us to put all this in context:

> *[23]Therefore, if you are offering your gift at the altar and there remember that your brother has something against you, [24] leave your gift there in front of the altar. First go and be reconciled to your brother; then come and offer your gift. (Matthew 5:23-24)*

This passage is important for Christians who are considering forgiving others or making amends. When we go to another person to offer them forgiveness or to make a direct amend, we are undertaking something of significant spiritual consequence. Both must be done with a pure heart and pure motives, not because it says that we *should* do it in this or any other book. If we are forgiving, we must do it with no strings attached; if we are asking for forgiveness, we need to expect nothing from the other person.

It is essential to keep in mind that we may have been damaged by someone or damaged others who are not in the same spiritual place that we are in today. They may not want to forgive us. They may not even accept the fact that they have done anything wrong to us. If we simply try to meet with them, write letters or make restitution, we might be creating new resentments instead of resolving issues of the past. If we have injured someone they may have good reason (in their humanness) not to forgive us unconditionally. Instead, we need to engage these people as partners in our search for accountability.

If we want to properly offer forgiveness to someone, we must adopt and make known a new set of boundaries or rules that will help insure that such an injury will not happen to us again and be able to live with who they are. Likewise, if someone is coming to us to ask for forgiveness, we need to able to ask them to provide us with boundaries that are based on accountability. This is especially vital if they wish to renew any kind of relationship with us. Making or accepting an apology does not mean putting yourself back in a place of risk.

God's direction and appropriate boundaries help us to be pure in our motives in both forgiving and in offering forgiveness. In our new life we do not want to create new conflicts over old behavior. This is why we need to do this in God's strength and not our own. We are asked to make amends (to set things at peace with others), except when to do so would create greater injury. It is God's desire that we be ready to forgive when the opportunity comes through doors that He opens, not the ones that we kick down. The peace that comes from being patient will allow us to grow faster in our faith and recovery.

> ³*David asked the Gibeonites, "What shall I do for you? How shall I make amends so that you will bless the LORD's inheritance?"*
> *(2 Samuel 21:3)*

Making direct amends has very little, if anything, to do with *apologizing* to people. It has very much to do with setting the past at peace. In fact, running to a person we have injured and explaining that we have come to a relationship with Christ and we want them to forgive us may be more hurtful and confusing to them than the original injury. The other side of this (from the perspective of someone who has been injured), would be us seeking out someone who had injured us and forcing them to apologize. Even if you extracted the apology from them, it would be of little value to you.

Instead, to truly make amends, we first need to offer people evidence of a changed heart. This involves who we are, what we do and how we do it. It involves not what we say, but what we do. When we understand that we properly make amends by first changing our own heart and our actions, we will then see what God wants us to do. (We can be rejected in making amends and still exactly be God wants us.)

"anonymity"
the spoken assurance that what we share in our circle of faith or accountability partner that stays with them and is not shared with others

Priorities that heal

God wants us to focus on healing, community, and life change. He wants us to let go of the things in our lives that are hurting us and tearing us to shreds. He wants us to set priorities that will both advance our healing and encourage the healing of those around us. If we have used pornography at the expense of our spouse; if we have manipulated and controlled; acted out in rage; acted out with food, drugs or alcohol or we have been damaged by another person, He wants us to embrace healing as a priority in our lives.

Matthew 5:23-24 asks those taking sacrifices to the altar to examine their motives for doing so. Are they doing it to look good or to heal and draw closer to God? Are they doing it because of their heart or a sense of duty and ritual? It goes further by asking that individual to act immediately or to set their misplaced priorities aside and take up the one that they should be focusing on… *healing*. Whatever we are trying to do in terms of making amends, we need to put it down until we are right with God and our offering is pure and consistent with what He wants us to bring as a gift.

Christ asks us to establish and reconnect in community based on our desire to heal the wounds of our past. People often stop coming to churches because the priority is not healing. They often stop because words are said that injure them or advice given is not of God. But, if we are in a true Christ-centered community, we can listen and share our experience, strength and hope as we help each other heal in God's power.

It is a spiritual battle

In the Christian life, we are fighting a spiritual battle.

> *[12] For our struggle is not against flesh and blood, but against the rulers, against the authorities, against the powers of this dark world and against the spiritual forces of evil in the heavenly realms. (Ephesians 6:12)*

We need to recognize that any meaningful ground gained in our spiritual growth will be hard fought and not taken in our own power. When we are making breakthroughs we may be attacked at work, attacked in our relationships, and attacked in those areas of our lives that are open to negative influence. It is satan's hope that he can discourage us from finding a personal relationship with Jesus Christ and keep us away from others of faith who can help us to be victorious. satan wants us isolated and alone!

But you are not alone

When we made our decision to turn our will and our lives over to the care of God, we did it for a very good reason. He has created the entire earth and everything on it, parted seas, defeated armies, calmed storms, and breathed life into all living things. Most importantly, He defeated death so that we might live eternally and so that the Holy Spirit could be with us in community with others. Consider the following passage…

> *⁷Dear friends, let us love one another, for love comes from God. Everyone who loves has been born of God and knows God. ⁸Whoever does not love does not know God, because God is love. ⁹This is how God showed his love among us: He sent his one and only Son into the world that we might live through him. ¹⁰This is love not that we loved God, but that he loved us and sent his Son as an atoning sacrifice for our sins. ¹¹Dear friends, since God so loved us, we also ought to love one another. (1 John 4:7-11)*

It is for this reason that we need to come together as a community of believers not to judge each other, but to love and support one another. This process asks us to take our inventory and become comfortable with sharing who we really are. This is a way of defeating satan's plan to isolate us in our guilt and shame. satan wants us alone so he can work on us. To win in this spiritual battle, we need to seek the company of others who are in Christ.

> *¹⁶Therefore confess your sins to each other and pray for each other so that you may be healed. The prayer of a righteous man is powerful and effective. (James 5:16)*

> *⁸Be self-controlled and alert. Your enemy the devil prowls around like a roaring lion looking for someone to devour. (1 Peter 5:8)*

Lions, wolves and tigers all hunt in the same way. They find a herd of animals, look for the weak and the stragglers, then separate them from the herd. Once you are separated from the support and strength of fellow believers, you are open for attack. satan uses separation, time and lies to try to isolate you permanently. How do we fight this?

- Go to meetings faithfully with other believers seeking the truth. Don't isolate.
- Work with an accountability partner.
- Get involved in service.
- Come in gratitude, joy, and prayer.
- Read God's word each day and pray for direction.

Community is created when we are involved in service. When we are, it is far less likely that we will say to ourselves that we don't need to go or that we feel too tired to go. It is on those days that satan is most earnestly attacking us and hoping we won't go. By not giving in to selfishness we will have already defeated him by being in service of others!

We are not built to undertake this journey of faith by ourselves. By finding a community of believers, you'll have someone to call when you are alone and hurting. We need to stop being loners who are afraid of letting other people or God get close to us. We need to let our guard down a little and open ourselves up to the encouragement and honesty of relationships that are built on something other than drinking, overeating, overworking, raging, drugs, fixing people or acting out sexually. To get to this place of real healing we need the help of others and they need you. You become part of a powerful ministry when you allow God to use you in a community. Let Him use you as a blessing to others.

"progress not perfection"

a constant reminder that we need to see our recovery work in faith as a journey not a destination... and that only Christ was perfect

Another former small group participant describes a meeting he once attended:

> "When I first came into recovery I went to a meeting that only had one other person in it. He was the only one that I could turn to as a sponsor. He had different habits than I did, I was young; he was old, I was single; he was married. He hated young punks that thought they knew it all; I thought he was arrogant, opinionated, and always needed to have the last word. I had asked him for help because I didn't like myself or anything that I was doing. Even though I didn't like him at first, I later came to respect him as God used our relationship to help me get through the first few months of my recovery. His witness led me to a relationship with Christ. He was truly a Godsend.
>
> Bob taught me one of the most important things I have ever learned in recovery… that we react with the highest degree of anger and frustration to the failures in others that also reside within us."

Relationships are important to healing and recovery. Look for a person of faith (same sex) who you can rely on to listen to you (and not try to fix you) and share their own experience strength and hope. You don't have to like them, just the way they walk with Christ. Listen for how and what they share in meetings and watch what they do. When you find someone that you think can help you, don't hesitate to ask them for that help. Set up some ground rules, like who calls who, how many times a week, where you will meet and what you will review. Be sure that you have more than one person so that when one is not available you still have others to call on. It is next to impossible to come to a new life and to sustain that change without other seekers of God's truth around you.

1. What community do you now have around you? Who can you count on in your walk of faith?

_____

_____

_____

_____

2. What injury has been done to you that you need to forgive?

_____

_____

_____

_____

Perspective for forgiveness

Prior to his conversion, the apostle Paul helped kill Stephen, one of the most committed followers of Jesus. We can assume that Stephen was loved by Peter because he was chosen by the early leaders of the church to help deal with the needs of the poor. It is hard when someone attacks you, but when they injure loved ones it can take resentment to a whole new level. Paul had been a religious zealot who rejected Christ and a murderer who wanted to destroy the church. Did Peter personally forgive Paul?

> *14So then, dear friends, since you are looking forward to this, make every effort to be found spotless, blameless and at peace with him. 15Bear in mind that our Lord's patience means salvation, just as our dear brother Paul also wrote you with the wisdom that God gave him. (2 Peter 3:14-15)*

Peter did not blindly open his life to someone who was driven by rage and violence. Rather, he saw within Paul real life change based on his *actions* not just his words. Only then did he count him an ally and a brother in Christ. Peter and Paul together became driving forces in the establishment of the early church. When we set our differences aside, ask for and receive forgiveness using God's power and not our own, we can build an authentic Christian community anywhere and with anyone.

> *17Do not repay anyone evil for evil. Be careful to do what is right in the eyes of everybody. 18 If it is possible, as far as it depends on you, live at peace with everyone. 19Do not take revenge, my friends, but leave room for God's wrath, for it is written: "It is mine to avenge; I will repay," says the Lord. (Romans 12:17-19)*

If we are harboring resentment, holding on to anger or seeking revenge for injury caused to us, we remove God's power and love from the picture. We must understand that God is in control and turn the situation over to Him. This allows us to be pure in our motives to forgive and to offer forgiveness knowing that a price was paid for us. God is more than able and will provide for us in this area of our faith if and when we are prepared to give it to Him. He is less interested in our sacrifices than He is with our hearts and our desire to rebuild and strengthen one another. Even if there is injury, even if there has been huge damage done, the test on both sides of the issue is always of our hearts.

> *28Later, knowing that all was now completed, and so that the Scripture would be fulfilled, Jesus said, "I am thirsty." 29A jar of wine vinegar was there, so they soaked a sponge in it, put the sponge on a stalk of the hyssop plant, and lifted it to Jesus' lips. 30When he had received the drink, Jesus said, "It is finished." With that, he bowed his head and gave up his spirit. (John 19: 28-30)*

At the end of his suffering, humiliation, and pain Jesus wanted to make sure that yet one more chance was given to anyone who was searching for truth. He did it in the hope that

---

"stinking thinking" when we don't return to our former habits, but to the attitudes that accompanied them... for example, we don't overeat any longer but still become short-tempered and isolate the same way we did when we did overeat

even in His final act of submission that He might reach one more person. He gave everything so that we could count on His forgiveness. When we hold onto the pain, resentment and anger and do not seek to restore to faith those we have injured or those who have injured us, *we discount the pain of Christ's sacrifice*. If there was ever anyone who walked this earth who had grounds for justifiable resentment, it was Jesus. Instead, He chose to forgive and offer the means by which every one of us can be forgiven.

Devotional Verse

Make and receive amends, do it in God's strength and love and find a new place of peace in your life. Read Psalm 69:13-21. This passage gives us insight into the pain endured and the price paid so we could have community and forgiveness through the suffering of Christ.

More questions for reflection

3. Are you discounting the sacrifice of Christ by not forgiving or offering forgiveness? If so, how are you doing that?

_____

_____

_____

_____

_____

4. Is there someone in your life who you need restore your relationship with, but have not because of the hardness of your heart or your desire to judge them?

_____

_____

_____

_____

_____

5. Have you ever been guilty of judging, gossiping, and dividing the community that God wants you to find healing and heal others in? If so, give an example.

___

6. What has been the outcome of you holding on to bitterness, resentment, and pain?

___

7. Are you praying for the strength to forgive? If so what are you praying?

___

Journaling Space:

vigilance

we continued to take personal inventory measured by our faith in God and when we make mistakes, we promptly admit them...

Read: 1 Kings 19:9-21 (Watching for God)

vig·i·lance: noun
(Dictionary): alert watchfulness
(Faith): maintain our focus on what heals us

The language of healing and recovery often runs counter to many of the words that we've heard used throughout our lives. Many of us have become more familiar with a language of fear, doubt, confusion, anger, and mistrust. But now, we have come to understand and overcome the obstacle of denial by seeking healing; we have come to trust God and turned our will and our lives over to His care; we have just completed the task of separating ourselves from the past by doing our inventory, and humbly asking God to remove our shortcomings. We have also become willing to make and accept amends. Having come this far in our word study, we should be seeing some changes in the way we think about these terms. By now, you've probably noticed that these words can be divided into three groups:

Those that Deal with our Faith
Denial, Seek and Trust. Overcoming denial requires the faith to admit we cannot change our lives by ourselves. Seeking God requires the faith to search and trust requires the faith to turn our will and lives over to His care.

Those that Deal with Taking Action
Fearless, Forgiven, Transform, Miracle, Relationship and Community. Each requires an action. Instead of sitting around and complaining about our circumstances, we become active and engaged in God's process for changing our lives. (The action part must be taken from God's direction.) We are asking for God's help to change. We actively seek out those who we have hurt or deal with the emotional baggage from hurt at the hands of others. Like the parting of the Red Sea, God is making us a path. We need to walk through it.

Those that Deal with our Growth
Vigilance, Power, and Share. Each word represents one of the three final steps in growing into people of strong and resilient faith. Without spiritual growth at this stage (or any stage of our healing) we will fall right back to the place that created our despair. In order to carry on in strength, sustain true growth and maintain our peace, we must be vigilant. We must maintain our focus on what heals us and makes us better versus slipping back into the turmoil of the past. When we use things other than God to fill ourselves up, to solve our problems or to quench our thirst, we will not only fail to grow, but begin to backslide away from the love of God that is always available to us. For example, if we fall into a pattern of

"intervention"
the coming together of concerned individuals who want to confront and offer solutions to someone who is struggling with an issue that is destroying their life and/or the lives of those around them

codependency or people pleasing at an early age, we will react emotionally to issues at that same age level until we identify and address the problem using God's wisdom and strength. Then and only then can we grow. Therefore, understanding the concept of vigilance helps us to shift our focus and stay the course, so that we don't return to actions of our past.

Biblical reference

Vigilance must be taken seriously. We must understand that we are in a spiritual battle for our heart, mind, and soul. This chapter's reference shows us there is a lot at stake here, regardless of where we are in our study or spiritual growth.

> *¹For I do not want you to be ignorant of the fact, brothers, that our forefathers were all under the cloud and that they all passed through the sea. ²They were all baptized into Moses in the cloud and in the sea. ³They all ate the same spiritual food ⁴and drank the same spiritual drink; for they drank from the spiritual rock that accompanied them, and that rock was Christ. ⁵Nevertheless, God was not pleased with most of them; their bodies were scattered over the desert.*
>
> *⁶Now these things occurred as examples to keep us from setting our hearts on evil things as they did. ⁷Do not be idolaters, as some of them were as it is written: "The people sat down to eat and drink and got up to indulge in pagan revelry." ⁸We should not commit sexual immorality, as some of them did—and in one day twenty-three thousand of them died. ⁹We should not test the Lord, as some of them did—and were killed by snakes. ¹⁰And do not grumble, as some of them did—and were killed by the destroying angel. ¹¹These things happened to them as examples and were written down as warnings for us, on whom the fulfillment of the ages has come. ¹²So, if you think you are standing firm, be careful that you don't fall! ¹³No temptation has seized you except what is common to man. And God is faithful; he will not let you be tempted beyond what you can bear. But when you are tempted, he will also provide a way out so that you can stand up under it. ¹⁴Therefore, my dear friends, flee from idolatry. (I Corinthians 10:1-14)*

In this passage, Paul is trying to warn the church at Corinth and all the rest of us as well. This letter was written to believers who had seen the miraculous growth and incredible excitement of the early church. But with that, they had also seen terrible persecution, pain, and extreme difficulty. Paul is encouraging them to understand the depth of the battle, to seek Christ's support in it and look to Him for a way out.

Paul goes on to remind us about how God provided for the children of Israel in the desert. Paul describes how the Lord led them through the parted waters of the Red Sea; and how God guided them across the desert with a pillar of smoke in the day and another of fire at night. Paul put this daily provision of God into the context of the miracles that God performed to show His followers that He is the true and living God to be reckoned with.

Paul also lists those things that we need to be vigilant about. These should convict everyone who is trying to honestly walk in faith. He lists sexual sin and immorality; the worship of idols that we construct with our hands or in our hearts; as well as gluttony and drunkenness. Paul warns about blindly accepting things the world tells us bring pleasure versus embracing the things that God wants for us. Then Paul adds one more thing that will include anyone of us who is not yet guilty of something else on the list… grumbling.

Paul further warns that seeing the miracles, feeling the presence of God, and experiencing life change will not totally sustain us. It is our vigilance, our desire to see God for who He is, not with the eyes that we use for reading this book, but with the *eyes of our heart*. When we are seeking to stay right with God through daily examination of our heart, we exercise vigilance by keeping our eyes on our relationship with Christ. More specifically:

We Are Not Alone

One of the reasons we want to take a daily "heart inventory" is to make sure that we stay in a good place with our friends, family, and others. Whatever you are going through, you can take courage that someone in the Bible, someone in your family of believers or someone else you know has faced a similar problem or temptation. Not because misery enjoys company, but because their stories (like your new-found power of brokenness) are living testimonies of victory. We can show each other the way to achieve victory over the darkness in our lives if we are faithful to God's word. satan wants to isolate us from one another, focus on past mistakes and fear of the future in order to drive the peace of the Holy Spirit from us. Resist by staying in pure community with others.

God is Faithful

Paul asks us to trust in the faithfulness of God and believe that we do not seek change in vain. His timing is perfect, God is never late, never early and always on time. He promises to create good from the bad things people have done to us. God promises to complete us and give us the peace and the relationships that we desire if we will simply wait for His direction and trust in His wisdom and strength. Walking in faith and waiting for God to lead is one of the hardest things we do in this life. In our impatience, a lot of us "run out in front of the bus" and then get angry with God for not holding us back from our own stupidity. Even when we do that, He still loves us despite that shortcoming. He wants us to know that above and beyond all the circumstances of our lives, we can count on a relationship with Him. He will be faithful.

God Will Show Us a Way Out

When we make mistakes that affect our faith or our recovery, we need to remember this promise. No matter what you are working through in your life, God promises that when we are struggling or tempted, He will provide a way out for us. This promise applies not to just one specific problem or temptation, but to the complete restoration of peace and unity with Him in our lives regardless of how many mistakes we've made. If we continue to look vigilantly into our own hearts and promptly admit when we are wrong, God will show us a way if we are prepared to wait, listen, and act when we understand His will for us.

"step study"

a group established for the specific purpose of working people through the 12 steps in a predetermined time and with a curriculum that is laid out in advance

Questions for reflection

1. Do you have any unresolved conflicts or relationships that you need to promptly take responsibility for?

_____

_____

_____

_____

2. Are you being vigilant in the areas of your life that will help you to heal and lead you to a better understanding of who God is? What are those areas?

_____

_____

_____

_____

_____

3. Do you believe that God has a plan for your life and that He is faithful?

_____

_____

_____

_____

_____

4. Are you willing to take a daily "heart inventory" to stay in a healthy place with God, your friends, family, and others?

_____

_____

_____

_____

_____

_____

Devotional Verse

[20] My son, pay attention to what I say; listen closely to my words.
[21] Do not let them out of your sight; keep them within your heart;
[22] for they are life to those who find them and health to a man's whole body.
[23] Above all else, guard your heart, for it is the wellspring of life.
[24] Put away perversity from your mouth; keep corrupt talk far from your lips.
[25] Let your eyes look straight ahead, fix your gaze directly before you.
[26] Make level paths for your feet and take only ways that are firm.
[27] Do not swerve to the right or the left; keep your foot from evil.
(Proverbs 4:20-27)

Journaling Space:

power

we sought through daily prayer and meditation to improve our conscious contact with Christ, praying only for knowledge of His will for us and power to carry it out...

Read: Exodus 14:14-31 (The Lord will fight for you)

pow·er: noun
(Dictionary): strength or force exerted or capable of being exerted; the ability or official capacity to exercise control or authority
(Faith): dominion over all things or authority in Godliness that can never be challenged or overcome

When we make the decision to change, we often do it because we are sick and tired of the life that we have been living. That choice is usually based on an earnest desire to do things differently. However, under on our own strength, it doesn't always work out that way. Meaningful change is based upon something much stronger than our own self-will.

We live in a society that attempts to describe changed lives in terms of New Year's resolutions, self-help, and higher states of consciousness. On the other hand, biblically based healing leads to a different and more permanent kind of change, *change that comes from the inside out, not from the outside in*. Most of us have tried a number of different ways to achieve lasting change in our lives. We've bought the books, attended the seminars, and watched the TV shows. We've bravely fought our way through weeks, months, or years of self-inflicted pain, only to create even more chaos for ourselves and those around us. With all this failure in mind, how can we create real and enduring change in our lives?

The answer to this question lies in the source of power that we use to make the change. The only power that can overcome the pain of addiction, the devastation of divorce, the hurt of codependency or damage of any other human failing is the power of the living God. God is in the change business. Since the very beginning, He has been taking broken lives and turning them into success stories for the purposes of His kingdom. He has the ability to make all things work together for the good of those that place their faith in Him. God promises us that He can and will change our lives through His Holy Spirit. This is the true power of brokenness.

> *²⁶In the same way, the Spirit helps us in our weakness. We do not know what we ought to pray for, but the Spirit himself intercedes for us with groans that words cannot express. ²⁷And he who searches our hearts knows the mind of the Spirit, because the Spirit intercedes for the saints in accordance with God's will. ²⁸And we know that in all things God works*

"meeting"

an established place where we can come together to speak openly and in a safe environment about the issues we are dealing with in our lives. in a Christian context we may find this in our homes, in a church or in a basement. from a Christian standpoint, two or more gathered together in the name of Christ to speak openly about the issues that they face and would like to overcome

> *for the good of those who love him, who have been called according to his purpose. (Romans 8:26-28)*

The problem is how do we get to a place where we can have the faith to trust God to change our lives? Such change comes only when we have made a decision to turn away from those things that are destroying us and our relationship with Him. *God can only move when we begin to see the love He has for us and allow that to shape our daily actions.* At the same time, we can't allow ourselves to become discouraged by fear, guilt, or shame. Moving in such a negative spirit has a power of its own that will only cause us to turn back in defeat to the way things were before.

To really change our lives, we must replace the desire to live under our own power with faith in God's ability to finish the job. To accomplish this, we must acknowledge who God is and turn our will and our lives over to His care, not just intellectually, but as a lifestyle. Only then, can we look beyond the issues of the past and the fears of tomorrow and focus on God's ability to provide something truly miraculous for us today. satan wants us defeated in healing and recovery by keeping us focused on the tomorrow we can't see and the yesterday we can't change.

God wants us to accept the reality of His presence in our life and to practice walking in His strength. He wants us to trust Him so He can influence, guide, and shape our lives. The more time we spend cultivating a personal relationship with Jesus Christ the greater our power to change becomes. We can find endurance in pain; faith in fear; new life in places of death and His voice in silence if we practice listening to Him. When we can see the miracles of the living God, hear His voice, and walk in the direction He is calling, we can experience real growth and joy.

"Power" more fully defined

In biblical terms, we need to look at its Greek origins in the word *kratov* meaning:

1. Force, strength
2. Power, might, mighty with great power, or a mighty deed
3. Dominion

The Bible refers to a dominion or ruling ability that cannot be challenged; a power that covers all things; power that we can use to forever change our lives. How can we begin to plug into such awesome strength? By setting aside part of our day to prayerfully ask God for healing, growth, and change. When we ask for His direction, we will find Him faithful.

> *⁶Do not be anxious about anything, but in everything, by prayer and petition, with thanksgiving, present your requests to God. ⁷And the peace of God, which transcends all understanding, will guard your hearts and your minds in Christ Jesus. (Philippians 4:6-7)*

1. What specific issue(s) that you have been trying to overcome by yourself, could you pray about right now and turn over to God?

_____

_____

_____

_____

Biblical reference

We can use God's power to not just strengthen ourselves, but to create a conduit of truth and light that will influence those around us.

> *¹²Therefore, as God's chosen people, holy and dearly loved, clothe yourselves with compassion, kindness, humility, gentleness, and patience. ¹³Bear with each other and forgive whatever grievances you may have against one another. Forgive as the Lord forgave you. ¹⁴And over all these virtues put on love, which binds them all together in perfect unity. ¹⁵Let the peace of Christ rule in your hearts, since as members of one body you were called to peace. And be thankful. ¹⁶Let the word of Christ dwell in you richly as you teach and admonish one another with all wisdom, and as you sing psalms, hymns, and spiritual songs with gratitude in your hearts to God. ¹⁷And whatever you do, whether in word or deed, do it all in the name of the Lord Jesus, giving thanks to God the Father through him. (Colossians 3:12-17)*

"advice giving" giving unsolicited advice to others about what they should be doing to solve their problems... often referred to as "shoulding on someone"

At the time Paul wrote this, the Colossians where being persecuted, attacked, jailed, tortured, and even murdered for their faith. Despite their horrific persecution, the church grew and these people of God prospered. Have you ever wondered how it is possible that in the midst of such pain and harassment, the early church could actually flourish?

The Bible is filled with stories that can help us grow our belief in the power and majesty of God in times of difficulty and struggle. We can gain a better understanding of God's strength when we apply it in the middle of our weakness. One of our favorites is found in the books of Chronicles, Kings, and Isaiah. It records the conquests of Sennacherib, (sen- a-chair-ib) then King of Assyria, the most powerful nation in the world at that time. Sennacherib declared war on Judiah. The children of Israel watched helplessly as one of the largest armies in the history of the Middle East was sent to destroy their capital. In the face of what seems to be certain defeat, Hezekiah, (heze-ki-ah) reminds his people they will be protected by a power far greater than anything that the world can muster. Hezekiah tells the people:

> *⁷"Be strong and courageous. Do not be afraid or discouraged because of the king of Assyria and the vast army with him, for there is a greater power with us than with him. ⁸With him is only the arm of flesh, but with us is the LORD our God to help us and to fight our battles." And the people gained confidence from what Hezekiah the king of Judah said.*
> *(2 Chronicles 32: 7-8)*

Messengers of the Assyrian army went to the gates of the city and demanded they surrender. The men on the walls were told that all was lost and the city would be crushed. They let them know there was absolutely no hope, because their army had destroyed every other city that it had come against, including those far more fortified than Jerusalem. Every soldier there understood this to be true. When Hezekiah heard of this, he was filled with fear. But instead of creating his own battle plan, he decided to go to God in prayer. Hezekiah asked God to glorify Himself in the salvation of the city and His temple. Then he realized that Isaiah was in the city and went to him for a word from God. Isaiah gave him this from God:

> *³²"Therefore, this is what the LORD says concerning the king of Assyria: "He will not enter this city or shoot an arrow here. He will not come before it with shield or build a siege ramp against it. ³³By the way that he came he will return; he will not enter this city, declares the LORD. ³⁴I will defend this city and save it, for my sake and for the sake of David my servant." ³⁵That night the angel of the LORD went out and put to death a hundred and eighty-five thousand men in the Assyrian camp. When the people got up the next morning—there were all the dead bodies! ³⁶So Sennacherib king of Assyria broke camp and withdrew. He returned to Nineveh and stayed there. (2Kings 19:32-36)*

Not surprisingly, recent excavations of Nineveh have uncovered archeological evidence to support this defeat of the Assyrians. It would appear that God's answer was more than just a good story on trusting Him to defend his people! Are you one of God's people? Now is the time to stand in the promise of his protection. When we make the mistake of first turning to our own strength and not to God's power, we fail to take advantage of His promise to deliver us. When we use anger, violence, or isolation to try to solve our problems, we miss the opportunity not only to repair the situation, but to defeat the evil at the source of it. This is worth remembering when life comes at us all at once and we feel like we are being swept away into darkness.

2. Is God showing you His living power? Are you asking?

_____

_____

_____

_____

3. In the past, where did you find the power to get though daily life?

_____

_____

_____

_____

It is in the power of God's word (Christ), prayer and the company of God's people that miraculous change comes. When we pray for one another and spend time in God's word, He can destroy the things that seek to destroy us. Each time we are victorious in the power of God, we can help others defeat the things that are about to destroy them. It is our faith that attracts others when they see where we place our trust in the midst of the storm. When we trust in God based on His faithfulness in our lives and the lives of others, we can put His awesome power to work.

More questions for reflection

4. Do you trust God to help you with trouble? Can you use His power to rejoice in it?

_____

_____

_____

_____

5. When you find victory in life, who gets the credit for it?

_____

_____

_____

_____

6. Can you commit to reading God's word and asking for His power to fill your life every day?

_____
_____
_____
_____

7. When was the last time that you earnestly sought His support? What was the outcome?

_____
_____
_____
_____

share

having had a spiritual awakening, we carry the good news to others and practice these principles in all our affairs...

Read: 2 Corinthians 3:3 (Be a living testimony of Christ)

sha re: verb
(Dictionary): an equitable portion; to use, enjoy, or experience jointly or in turns
(Faith): to be filled by relating one's experience, strength, and hope to others

In this book it has been our goal to focus on twelve key words that represent the central themes of healing, not as defined by the world, but from a biblical standpoint. It is my hope that fully understanding these words will help you grow in your faith.

There are two extreme viewpoints in our modern world that repeatedly clash with each other. One is the notion that words, concepts and ideas represent only what you personally believe them to mean. In other words, where there is no absolute truth, only "relative truth" that one believes to be true in one's own mind. The opposing view holds that language allows us to communicate *things of absolute truth that never change.*

"unsafe person" someone who you are unable to speak to openly about issues you face for fear of gossip, belittling or even retribution

1. Have you seen anything that you can count on as absolutely true as it relates to your relationship with God?

_____

_____

_____

_____

If we feel there is no absolute truth, we can go through our entire life doing as we please, injuring and being injured, all while looking for someone else to blame. With this relative way of thinking, there is no predefined standard of right and wrong. This flawed reasoning often leads us to believe that we can't possibly be wrong, so we fester in our bitterness and isolation while looking for a scapegoat. We make bad decisions, suffer the consequences, and curse the raw deal the world is giving us. Then we blame our family, our job, our church and even God. What we don't look at is our own role in all of it.

David gives us a clear description of the thought process of those who reject the truth…

> *¹The fool says in his heart, "There is no God." They are corrupt, their deeds are vile; there is no one who does good. (Psalm 14:1)*

Very few people can honestly say they don't believe that God exists, but we often live as if He doesn't. But when things are not going our way, we shake our fists at Him in anger. We do not work with Him but blame Him for the outcome. The longer we fight to preserve our own definitions of truth and attempt to maintain control, the more energy we waste. When we go through life in ways that leave us feeling angry, isolated, and embittered, we can easily become spiritually weakened and separated from God. satan can then work to pull us even farther away; by having us focus on those things we hate not only about God, but about ourselves as well. By that point, we probably imagine that God hates us for our poor choices or just doesn't have time for us.

To defeat this destructive cycle in our lives, we must want positive change and seek out people who know that God can and will help us. When we seek healing in places of Christian fellowship, we will come to understand two things:

1.) *That our lives are unmanageable without God.* This is an eternal truth that we may reject for a time, but ultimately it will destroy us if we do not accept it.

2.) *That we are powerless without God.* When we try to make the rules and try to ignore the consequences, we are fighting against forces bigger than ourselves.

Absolute and eternal truth is the only thing upon which we can base our lives, faith, and healing. Without meaningful truth we have nothing. John recognizes this in the opening sentence of his record of the "good news" or gospel of faith in Christ...

> *¹In the beginning was the Word, and the Word was with God, and the Word was God. (John 1:1)*

In Greek, the primary word *logos* refers to a vessel for the conveyance of an idea (like a glass holds water). John tells us here that Christ was the vessel who conveyed the true idea of God to humanity. Christ reinforces this concept throughout the Gospels as He tells us who the Father is and what His kingdom is like.

> *⁹Jesus answered: "Don't you know me, Philip, even after I have been among you such a long time? Anyone who has seen me has seen the Father. How can you say, 'Show us the Father'?" (John 14:9)*

We do not have to understand the truth to understand that it exists, anymore than we need to understand the molecular structure of oxygen to breathe. When we make a choice to change our lives, we want to make the pursuit of truth and sharing it with others as natural as breathing!

A spiritual awakening

As we move our way through the process of healing and faith, we begin to focus more on who God is and to increasingly trust in His truth. When we do this, a spiritual awakening begins in us. We finally start to realize that trusting in our own power alone will lead us to emptiness, loss, and ruin.

For many of us, our definition of what it means to share comes from our experience in the world. In man's economy, what we give is divided and diminishes until there is nothing left. When we have a donut and we are asked to share, we have only the experience of giving up half a donut. In the world's view, we are emptied by giving.

In God's economy, we get filled up when we start to invest in or share with others. In Greek translations of the New Testament, one word that illustrates God's view of what it means to share is *antanaplhro*, (don't worry about pronouncing it!) meaning to "fill up in turn". We are filled by everything that we give away, share, or contribute under the spirit of God. But we can't assimilate this "filling" into our lives until we have had a true spiritual awakening. It is something we put into practice only by following through on the direction that He gives us, not because of our own guilt. For that, we look to God's word.

Biblical references

> *[18] Then Jesus came to them and said, "All authority in heaven and on earth has been given to me. [19] Therefore go and make disciples of all nations, baptizing them in the name of the Father and of the Son and of the Holy Spirit, [20] and teaching them to obey everything I have commanded you and surely I am with you always, to the very end of the age."*
> *(Matthew 28:18-20)*

This passage is commonly referred to as the Great Commission. The basis of the Lord's "marching orders" is His authority.

> *[20].....which he exerted in Christ when he raised him from the dead and seated him at his right hand in the heavenly realms, [21] far above all rule and authority, power and dominion, and every title that can be given, not only in the present age but also in the one to come. (Eph. 1:20-21)*

When we find good news we need to share it with others. When we see a need in others that resonates with us, we need to act on it. Regardless of how worthy or unworthy you feel, God can use you exactly where you are to help others, to grow their faith or to build a ministry. If you will simply share what you know about truth in your life, no matter how small it may seem to you, God will use it. He tells us this in the first chapter of James:

> *[22] Do not merely listen to the word, and so deceive yourselves. Do what it says. (James 1:22)*

"crosstalk"

in a recovery group, any conversation, action, or body language that communicates a message to another individual that excludes others ... it also can refer to interfering with the emotional sharing of another, even to the extent of handing them a tissue if they're crying

We see one of the clearest examples of this in the first chapter of the Book of John. Two young men seeking truth (Peter and Andrew) have been following John the Baptist. They are with John's disciples when they see Christ approaching. John the Baptist points to Jesus as the Messiah; the Savior he has been preparing his followers to meet. He then shares his testimony with all those who will listen. What unfolds is an example of a sharing that fills each life in a new and powerful way:

> *[40]Andrew, Simon Peter's brother, was one of the two who heard what John had said and who had followed Jesus. [41]The first thing Andrew did was to find his brother Simon and tell him, "We have found the Messiah" (that is, the Christ). [42]And he brought him to Jesus. Jesus looked at him and said, "You are Simon son of John. You will be called Cephas (Peter)".*
> *(John 1:40-42)*

John the Baptist had a spiritual awakening and shared the good news about the freedom that comes when we turn away from evil and follow Christ! He shares even though he knows that it could cost him his life. John's testimony is heard by two people that are not in a position of spiritual strength. They are simply seeking truth, and when they find it they go on to share that truth, not in their own power, but in the power of Christ Jesus.

The outcome of John the Baptist's sharing is the commitment of Andrew, (Christ's first disciple), and a life-change for Peter, who would become a huge force in the early Church. It is not simply about the witness of John, but the power that comes when we share our testimony with others. When we have the power of Christ in us, we will do more to further the kingdom and the cause of healing and recovery than we ever could by ourselves.

Truth is still truth, regardless of the size of the revelation. When we are prepared to share it in the same way that Christ was, God takes what we have and multiplies it to create something larger than we could ever dream of. Those of us with a background in traditional recovery groups like Alcoholics Anonymous (which has its original roots in Christianity) will be familiar with the concept of filling ourselves by sharing. There, they say "we only keep what we have by giving it away." As Christians, we know that these ideas are truly of God since they are not understandable in human terms.

Words that change lives

Those outside of the recovery movement often look at it with amazement, marveling at the degree of life change that it produces. How can sharing these twelve words change a person's life? The answer to this question is found by looking at the order and progression of the words, as they move us from brokenness and separation from God to a place where we have strength in Christ to share His good news with others. This process of healing is divinely inspired, orderly and biblical. As we seek healing, we seek God, separating ourselves from the issues of the past as we share our experience, strength, and hope with others. The more we share, the more we are filled. God is in the business of turning what appears to be nothing into something of great value.

It is this blending of brokenness and sharing that makes the Christian healing/recovery movement a place of revolutionary excitement within the Church. Christian recovery is not simply to be part of the Church, but what the Church must be about. It is exactly one's sharing in a body of believers that creates a place of hope for the lost in your neighborhood as well as for those who live in silent pain inside the church itself.

2. Have you had the experience of being filled as you shared faith with others?

_____

_____

_____

_____

_____

"sponsor"
a person of the same sex who we ask to assist us in completing the 12 steps of recovery who has worked those steps and has experienced life change as a result

In the language of healing, we use words to help us better understand the actions we take to find healing and to better share the good news with others. To grow in our recovery and our faith, we need to search for solid and deep meaning that will stand up against the assault of everyday life. To continue forward on our own journey and be a witness to others, we need to fully understand and embrace the message of the Gospel:

> *[28]...so Christ was sacrificed once to take away the sins of many people; and he will appear a second time, not to bear sin, but to bring salvation to those who are waiting for him. (Hebrews 9:28)*

The message is this... if we place our faith, our trust, and our lives in the hands of Jesus Christ we will be forgiven and a new life will begin. His sacrifice is enough to forgive us for any and every wrong that we have ever done or will ever do! This is how we are to share... by first accepting the forgiveness of God through His Son's death and resurrection and then sharing that hope with others through the life change that power brings. Not by telling people to stop what they are doing first and act in a certain way. Not by browbeating them for what they are not doing. Nor by telling them what they *should* be doing, but by non-judgmentally sharing our own experience, strength, and hope in Christ.

No matter where we are in our journey, it is critical that we understand Christ's message of forgiveness, mercy, and grace. If we accept and share the message of forgiveness, we will be able to overcome the grief, shame, fear, and guilt that are at the center of all relapses. These are the things that attack us in our new life; they keep us from finding freedom and drive us right back into all the garbage in our lives that we want so much to overcome.

More questions for reflection

3. Are you in a place right now where you are ready to share your own experience, strength, and hope with others?

_____

_____

_____

_____

_____

4. Are you prepared to share it with others right here, right now?

_____

_____

_____

_____

_____

5. What opportunities do you see for sharing in the near future?

_____

_____

_____

_____

_____

6. What, if anything, would stop you from sharing your experience, strength, and hope with others?

_____
_____
_____
_____
_____
_____

Where to go from here?

Biblically speaking, we can begin to prayerfully ask God to show us three new relationships.

The first of these will be a discipleship (Paul) type relationship with a person of faith who knows what it means to overcome great darkness in God's power. We want to seek the strength of their experience and their healing in Christ so that a new life can be discovered.

The second will be to find an encouraging relationship. This will be a person God can use in our lives to lift us up. It will be someone who we can trust to stand with us during difficult times as we seek true life change. Even miraculous life changes come with some tension. When God parted the Red Sea the Children of Israel were challenged in walking through it in faith.

Finally, we need to look for those who we can support on prayer and encourage them in their own journey of faith. We can refer to those as mentoring (Timothy) relationships. As soon as we find a new life in Christ, we have a testimony of faith to share. We can't give it in our own strength, but we can give it in His.

When we look at the lives of those who have time tested faith, those who have endured and overcome in God's power as part of our family, we will find the victory of love and encouragement and we will want to give back in His power. When we reach this point, we will have discovered the key to God's view of the Power of Brokenness and it will become part of our lives through Christ-centered community.

Journaling your thoughts...

By this time in your study, you have doubtless had a number of issues and feelings that have surfaced. Journaling helps you capture those thoughts in a way that you can look back at them days, weeks or even years later. Writing helps you process and clarify your innermost feelings. Here are some suggestions that will help get started keeping a journal:

What was good about today?

What was not so good about today?

How did I feel about what happened today?

What did I do to further develop my relationship with Jesus Christ?

How has God further revealed Himself to me today?

Some final thoughts...

Denial, Seek, Trust, Fearless, Forgiven, Transform, Miracle, Relationship, Community, Vigilance, Power, and Share. These are the twelve words or steps that lead us toward an understanding of the true power of brokenness. When we have opened ourselves up to admitting that we need to change the things in our lives that separate us from a fulfilling relationship with God, the change we seek will be close at hand. When we can begin to understand the great love that God has for us, that life change will soon become a part of who we are. When we turn our lives over to God, we will begin to see that it is more important to be who He wants us to be than how we see ourselves. When we walk in the power of the spirit of God, everything that we are and all we that we have can be used to build His kingdom.

We have now come to the end of this process from a book standpoint, but this should be only the beginning of a new and greater love affair with God. Spending as much time as we can in a daily time of prayer, study and being open to carry the message of hope to others, will help create a new spiritual strength in us. It will be a strength that will forever change the darkness and pain of our past into the light and power of our new present.

We are not called to be slaves to the pain of yesterday. Instead, we are asked to give Him all of our yesterdays, our hopes, our dreams, our fears, and our pain and allow Him to transform them. Once we understand that we are truly forgiven and that Christ came to set us free, we are free indeed. What we are called to is meeting with other believers, using that time to listen to God's voice and to share our experiences as testimonies to reach others.

You have within you, in the power of Christ, a message that changes lives. It is a power that rebuilds, heals, delivers, restores, and sets free. You can walk in the strength that parts seas, destroys evil, unites families, liberates churches and changes nations. You can use your voice in His strength to speak to all who will listen, not just about what you have been delivered from, but what you have been delivered for.

Share with those who are ready, not trying to make people ready if they are not willing to seek real life change. Walk in faith and expect adversity. It is in such adversity that we know that our sharing is effective. If we have no pain, we will have no ministry, and the process of separating ourselves from the garbage of our past will be stalled.

Finally, use the knowledge of your deliverance to ensure that the greatest joy and the greatest suffering create the same reaction to God. We are called to be people that do not live like the rest of the world. The pain in our lives, the trials and the injuries give us the opportunity to witness in a kind of power that most of the world does not yet understand. There will doubtless be times when the world will try to stop us from sharing what God has shown us, but if we are not anxious and wait on His direction, He will use us in mighty and powerful ways.

We pray that each person reading this book will find a new and living relationship with the word of God. We pray that there will be healing in your life and that you will find a new and meaningful power in brokenness. When they ask you why you do what you do, tell them Christ spoke these words to His church (synagogue) at the beginning of His ministry.

[18] "The Spirit of the Lord is on me, because he has anointed me to preach good news to the poor. He has sent me to proclaim freedom for the prisoners and recovery of sight for the blind, to release the oppressed, [19] to proclaim the year of the Lord's favor." [20] Then he rolled up the scroll, gave it back to the attendant and sat down. The eyes of everyone in the synagogue were fastened on him, [21] and he began by saying to them, "Today this scripture is fulfilled in your hearing." (Luke 4: 18-21)

The Serenity Prayer
*God grant me the serenity
to accept the things I cannot change;
courage to change the things I can;
and wisdom to know the difference.
Living one day at a time;
Enjoying one moment at a time;
Accepting hardships as the pathway to peace;
Taking, as He did, this sinful world
as it is, not as I would have it;
Trusting that He will make all things right
if I surrender to His Will;
That I may be reasonably happy in this life
and supremely happy with Him
Forever in the next.
Amen.*

Blessings,

Glen Kerby and Jim McCraigh

Leader's Guide for Conducting a Power Of Brokenness Circle

Circle meetings can take place in one hour or less. They can be held immediately before or after your regular church service time. To begin, have all participants first meet in one large circle then break into smaller groups later as noted below.

1. Open in prayer, praying earnestly and in the spirit for direction and healing. If there are any announcements, make sure that anything that you communicate has a strong biblical basis for being announced.
2. As a circle leader, introduce yourself and explain your role in the group and why you are leading. Explain what God is doing in your life and what your hope is for everyone who participates. Consider rotating this leadership role from week to week.
3. Talk about the group and ensure that all people attending are in the right place. The only requirement for participation is a desire to strengthen one's relationship with Christ.
4. Take time to do a separate small group or one-on-one time with new attendees so that they can be quickly brought up to speed. Ensure that you understand where a new person is coming from. Some people need badly to be in group settings the first time they attend and oriented after group, but others need the assurance of the group structure so that they can be comfortable in that group.
5. As needed, gently restore people who are using the time to preach, cross talk (engage in one-on-one dialogue at the expense of all others in the group that is not directed by the Holy Spirit), or those attempting to fix or give advice within the group.
6. Prompt open discussion by introducing a topic or personal testimony, tying that Sunday's message to a particular chapter heading in the book or by reviewing the Bible study notes within the chapters. This should take only 20-25 minutes at most.
7. At this time, if you have more than 4 or 5 in your larger circle, break into smaller groups for another 25 - 30 minutes after your open discussion or teaching time. The smaller and more intimate the groups are, the better the sharing will be. This also allows for those who are developing their gifts in leadership to start by leading smaller groups. Gender should not be a factor in that larger circle open teaching time but should be considered in group sharing times. You may find doing open sharing in a larger group with both men and women from time to time to be refreshing and fulfilling, for the most part it is much easier for women or men to open up about issues in their lives when same sex participants only surround them.
8. Close with prayer. Ask if specific healing is needed. Be prepared to listen to God's spirit and seek His will in that prayer time. Deep, intentional, and focused prayer time is key to healing. Do a time of open prayer and offer people the freedom to stay for a more personal and directed time of prayer. Ask for formal prayer requests and pray for one another during the week. Encourage additional Bible study time that unifies the group between meetings. Make it a point to ask circle members to reach out to others who might benefit from joining or starting their own Power of Brokenness group in another church.
9. Create and distribute phone lists of those willing to supply contact information so fellowship time, accountability and sponsorship opportunities can be formed outside of the meeting. The real work of church doesn't happen in a meeting, it happens afterward. Encourage participants to continue meeting with one another in fellowship time. Consider hosting events, barbeques, or coffee times to support them in doing that.
10. Ask participants to think about service opportunities in the ministry. Have a list of service needs available so that people can give of themselves. Selfishness is at the root of all of the sins that we struggle with. We need to give everyone a chance to defeat personal selfishness.
11. Follow up with those who miss circle meetings to ensure they are well. Group leaders should keep an active phone list in place and follow up with people that miss two consecutive meetings to find out if they are in need of support.
12. Regularly bring group leaders together monthly for encouragement, support and to respond to any questions and concerns that will come up in any front-line ministry.

How to Form Power of Brokenness Circles

The Power of Brokenness was written to help you gain greater insight into God's plan for miraculous life change. It can be used as a personal Bible study, a 12-week small group curriculum, or a step study mentoring guide. Some group leaders use it as a series of twelve teaching outlines prior to open sharing time that we call circles. But, no matter how you use it, there is only one requirement for true life change. The entire process must be submitted to Christ.

Throughout its pages, it is our intention to continually point you to Jesus Christ and to encourage further study of scripture. Without His Spirit in control of our time together, there can be no true healing. Putting Christ first in all things is important for creating an environment in which we can share, heal, pray (and be prayed for) and experience the miracle of His divine action in our lives.

Acting in the fruit of the spirit, as in Galatians 5:22-26, (see opposite page) and praying constantly for unity, harmony and divine assistance are the keys to forming a biblically based circle. When two or more of us come together, as those who seek a new way of living under Christ, we become a church. This church formation happens regardless of our location, size, or background. When we are gathered in Christ's name, we become part of His body. Any non-scriptural ideas, man-made rules, or non-biblical guidelines that we create in church or small group settings will always lead us away from God's truth and move us toward division or injury.

Leading people to a place of transparency can create emotional and spiritual challenges, therefore we need to maintain order in all that we do based on His Holy Spirit and not on the making of rules and religious frameworks. We need to encourage people to share based on what God is doing in their lives and what they desire to change.

Here are a few important small group guidelines to help you along the way, each based on the direction we get in Galatians about how to be a church:

1. **Christ** is the most important person in any circle or group. We must ensure that our group time is open and submitted to Christ, that we continually ask for His wisdom, and that we ensure that His inspiration is part of our group time. When we are led by the Holy Spirit to pray for someone or an issue in the group, if knowledge is given to us for our lives (or the lives of others) we must apply these biblically based gifts without fear or reservation. When we allow God to lead our group experience, we may begin to see things happen that may be out of the ordinary church experience. God is a God of love and a God of order. Do not let group time descend into unstructured chaos, but by the same token, do not be afraid for there to be freedom within the group for God to show us who He is. Christ promised us as believers that when we gather in groups of two or more, that He would be in the midst of us. Give Him a chance to speak. Select people to lead your group who are filled with God's Holy Spirit, who have strong spiritual gifts and who can be Christ-like in their leadership. Our job in healing is not to know things, but to know Christ. When we trust in His power to heal and are prepared to put forth the effort of discipleship, we will see His awesome power move in our lives.

2. **Love** is the filter through which all ideas of group time, sharing, structure and discipline must pass. Circle time must always be based on love. Any non-scriptural ideas about running group time, no matter how practical they may seem, must be rejected in love. God may put people in your life who are difficult to love but pray that you can act in love at all times and use conflict resolution skills given to us by Christ in Matthew 18. Love one another by being in love with each other, regardless of background, personality, issues, or struggles. Remember that many people will come into the center of our church families or circles who have never experienced real love and acceptance. We are in a spiritual battle against an enemy who is confused by love, confuse him by loving constantly!

3. **Joy** in all things is a pathway to finding a deeper more meaningful relationship with Christ. The spirit in which we come together will influence the success of our small group time as we try to grow in our relationship with Christ. If we meet in a spirit of religion, it will be rules and pain that will dominate our experience. If we meet in a critical spirit, we will produce a group that will likely be divided and critical. But if we meet in a spirit of joy, God can use us, speak to us, and work through us in unique and powerful ways.

4. **Peace** requires that all of the disputes that we have with others be put to rest immediately. This requires both vigilance and action based in love. When someone is acting out or causing issues during group time, that individual must be quickly and gently restored so the peace of the group can be maintained. This acting out will most often take the form of a group member talking about everyone else's problems except their own or people using religious ideas to judge others within the group. Maintaining peace demands that we not gossip in our circle time and that we will not judge one another in these group settings. (It is only if someone asks you to disciple or sponsor them, that you have been given license to privately speak into their lives in such an intimate way.) Lastly, when an individual comes to a circle and avoids talking about anything personal, you can be assured that they are not at peace. If we as leaders can ask them to share on why they are there, what they are feeling or what they see God doing in their lives, we can begin to see something miraculous happen.

5. **Patience** will allow us to stop and ask for God's direction when problem solving. Remember that He can and will protect His church if we will simply wait for Him and not act out of our flesh. There are only two spirits we can act in, His Spirit or the spirit of the world. Patience, personally and with one another, is one of the greatest weapons we have to destroy our human tendency to act in the spirit of the world. There is no room for rash or emotionally driven response in a small group environment if we want the Holy Spirit to dominate.

6. **Kindness** means taking action. When we act in kindness, open up in kindness, or rebuke in kindness, we bring restoration, joy, and hope to people. As circle leaders we want to speak words of life and encouragement into group member's lives. Kindness must always be our first response to the unkind.

7. **Goodness** is at the heart of the character of Christ. Goodness demands that we come together with Christ's ability to heal as the constant measure of our actions as people. To help to meet the needs of those within our circle, we can best help others by openly and transparently sharing our testimony of faith. We model this by sharing our experience, strength and hope and how we ourselves have been healed or are healing through God's goodness and grace.

8. **Faithfulness** is required of us in order to have a safe place to share and grow. We want to come to a place in our lives where what we have done and who we are becomes part of our public testimony of faith. Being full of faith means that we have totally placed our trust in things (of God) that are unseen by others. It is not usually part of the human condition to admit our failures openly. This is because others in the world may want to try to use our failures against us or to attack us in those places of weakness. But our faithfulness as believers allows us to share openly and trust that the outcome will build God's kingdom and help us to find healing, even if someone else tries to use our faith against us. Faithfulness also demands that we are good stewards of the information that we are given. We must ensure that when we share with one another that our information is given in the confidence of faith.

9. **Self-Control** is a key to ensuring that all of the other components of the fruit of the spirit are working. We may think that we have the right to tell someone else what they should or should not be doing. If that information is not guided by Biblical thought (or the Holy Spirit confirmed by scripture) then we are not exercising self-control. If we become frustrated with another person in our circle and act out in that, we are not acting in the Spirit and have lost our self-control. If we dominate sharing time; talk for longer than 3-5 minutes; use coarse language or fight over doctrinal positions, we are not exercising self-control. Every moment we waste talking about religious ideas is a moment stolen from us in discovering who Christ is.

Made in the USA
Las Vegas, NV
18 August 2024

94049528R00070